French
Revision

Julie Goodbourn

Contents

Lonely hearts

my name is

I am fifty years old

I live in a large house

Je m'appelle Ralph et j'ai cinquante ans. J'habite dans une grande maison. Je suis sympa, beau et grand. J'ai les yeux verts et les cheveux courts et gris.

my daughter

a lot

J'adore ma fille, Isabella. Elle est belle, amusante et intelligente. Je déteste ses copains. J'aime beaucoup mon petit chien, Spotless, et la musique classique. Je n'aime pas la télévision et je préfère le calme!

her friends

dog

peace and quiet

Vocab file

j'aime *I like*
je n'aime pas *I don't like*
j'adore *I adore/I love*
je déteste *I hate*
je préfère *I prefer*

je suis *I am*
amusant(e) *funny*
beau/belle *good-looking*
grand(e) *tall*
intelligent(e) *intelligent*
petit(e) *small*
sympa *nice*

j'ai *I have*
les yeux verts *green eyes*
les yeux marrons *brown eyes*
les cheveux courts *short hair*
les cheveux longs *long hair*
les cheveux gris *grey hair*
les cheveux blonds *blonde hair*
les cheveux roux *red hair*

Key facts

Comment t'appelles-tu?/Tu t'appelles comment? *What's your name?*
Je m'appelle *My name is*
Quel âge as-tu/Tu as quel âge? *How old are you?*
J'ai ... ans *I'm years old*
Où habites-tu? *Where do you live?*
J'habite... *I live...*
Tu es comment? *What are you like?*

Key facts

- **French nouns** are either masculine or feminine. It is a good idea to learn every new noun with the correct word for 'a' or 'the'. It will generally be **un** or **le** for masculine nouns and **une** or **la** for feminine nouns.

  un chien   a dog   **une** maison   a house
  le copain   the friend (male)   **la** musique   the music

- **French adjectives** (words for describing) have different endings depending on whether that person or thing is masculine or feminine, singular or plural.

  Feminine adjectives have an **e** at the end, and plural adjectives have an **s** at the end:

  amusant → amusants   amusante → amusantes

Matching pictures

Look at the pictures and decide who is saying each of the following sentences. Antoine or Laura? Write A or L for each one.

1 J'ai les yeux bleus.
2 J'adore mon petit chien.
3 Je déteste les cheveux courts.
4 J'ai les cheveux bruns et courts.
5 J'ai les cheveux blonds et frisés.
6 J'aime beaucoup la musique pop.

Laura   Antoine

Fill in the gaps

A spilt bottle of water has smudged some of this letter; can you fill in the missing words?

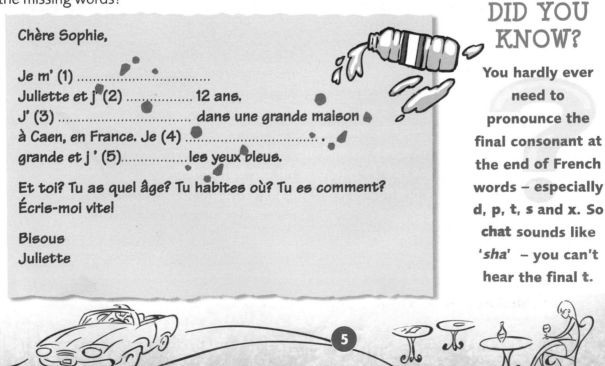

Chère Sophie,

Je m' (1) ....
Juliette et j' (2) .... 12 ans.
J' (3) .... dans une grande maison
à Caen, en France. Je (4) ....
grande et j' (5)................les yeux bleus.

Et toi? Tu as quel âge? Tu habites où? Tu es comment?
Écris-moi vite!

Bisous
Juliette

DID YOU KNOW?

You hardly ever need to pronounce the final consonant at the end of French words – especially d, p, t, s and x. So **chat** sounds like '*sha*' – you can't hear the final t.

Meet the family

Je m'appelle Max et j'habite dans une grande maison avec Ralph et Izzy. Je travaille pour la famille. J'ai quarante ans.

I work for

my boss

he's an inventor

a little eccentric

Ralph, mon patron, est très intelligent. C'est un inventeur, alors il est un peu excentrique. Il a cinquante ans.

a boyfriend

Sa fille s'appelle Isabella. Elle n'a pas de frères et sœurs. Elle est fille unique. Elle est jeune et belle et, comme son père, elle est très intelligente. Elle a un petit ami qui s'appelle Thomas.

he's sweet and never nasty

Le chien de la famille s'appelle Spotless. Il a cinq ans, il est mignon et jamais méchant. Malheureusement, il a tendance à faire des bêtises.

he has a tendency to misbehave

Vocab file

ma famille *my family*
ma mère *my mother*
ma belle-mère *my stepmother*
mon père *my father*
mon beau-père *my stepfather*
mon frère *my brother*
mon demi-frère *my half-/stepbrother*

ma sœur *my sister*
ma demi-sœur *my half-/stepsister*
mes frères et sœurs *my brothers and sisters*
mon grand-père *my grandfather*
ma grand-mère *my grandmother*
mon oncle *my uncle*
ma tante *my aunt*
mon cousin *my cousin (male)*
ma cousine *my cousin (female)*

avoir _to have_

You need to learn this verb as it will come in useful in all sorts of ways. It's an irregular verb; it doesn't follow the regular pattern of many French verbs.

j'ai _I have_   **nous avons** _we have_   **ils/elles ont** _they have_

tu as _you have_   **vous avez** _you have_   **on a** _we have_

il/elle a _he/she has_

Key facts

Make sure you understand and can use the following phrases.

As-tu des frères et sœurs? _Have you got any brothers and sisters?_

j'ai un frère _I've got one brother_

j'ai une sœur _I've got one sister_

je suis fils/fille unique _I'm an only child_

il/elle a ... ans _he/she is ... years old_

il/elle s'appelle... _his/her name is..._

ils/elles s'appellent... _they are called..._

il/elle habite... _he/she lives..._

ils/elles habitent... _they live..._

il/elle est beau/belle _he/she is good-looking_

Who is it?

Find out who they are talking about.

1 Il a quarante ans, il habite avec papa et moi et il travaille pour nous.

Il s'appelle

....

2 Elle a quatorze ans. Elle est fille unique. Je l'adore!

Elle s'appelle

....

3 Il a cinq ans et il est mignon.

Il s'appelle

....

4 Il est très sympa et il a une fille qui s'appelle Izzy.

Il s'appelle

....

DID YOU KNOW?

The -ent at the end of the **ils/elles** form of most verbs is silent.
In the sentences below, **s'appelle** and **s'appellent** sound the same,
you don't say the -ent.
So do **habite** and **habitent**, as well as **adore** and **adorent**.

Elle **s'appelle** Izzy.   _Her name is Izzy._

Ils **s'appellent** Ralph et Max.   _Their names are Ralph and Max._

Elle **habite** avec son père.   _She lives with her father_

Ils **habitent** dans une grande maison.   _They live in a big house._

Elle **adore** son père.   _She loves her dad._

Ils **adorent** Spotless.   _They love Spotless._

How many rooms?

Devoirs   le 5 mai 2005

Bonjour, je m'appelle Izzy et j'habite dans une grande maison près de Londres. Chez moi, il y a dix chambres, cinq salles de bains, deux salons, une grande salle à manger, une grande cuisine et un jardin énorme.

homework

near London

in my home

there are

Dans ma chambre il y a un lit, une armoire, une chaise et une table. Sous mon lit, il y a mon chien, Spotless, qui déteste les douches!

under

who hates showers

Vocab file

une chambre *bedroom*	une chaise *chair*
une cuisine *kitchen*	une commode *chest of drawers*
un garage *garage*	des étagères (f) *shelves*
un jardin *garden*	un frigo *fridge*
une pièce *room*	une lampe *lamp*
une salle à manger *dining room*	un lavabo *basin*
une salle de bains *bathroom*	un lit *bed*
un salon *living room*	un mur *wall*
une armoire *wardrobe*	un ordinateur *computer*
un bureau *desk*	des rideaux (m) *curtains*
un canapé *sofa*	une télé *TV set*

What goes where?

Read the words in the box and draw arrows to show which item goes in which room. (Some items can go in more than one room.)

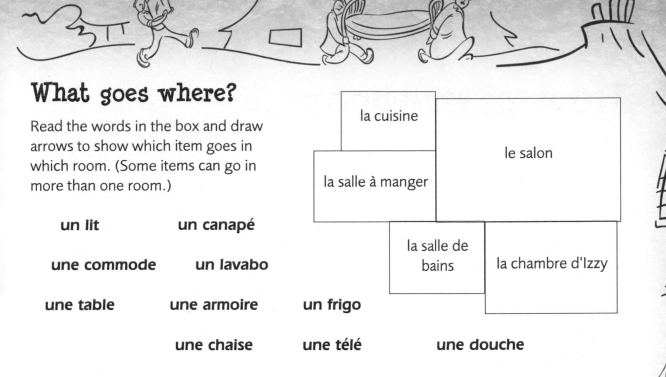

un lit   un canapé

une commode   un lavabo

une table   une armoire   un frigo

une chaise   une télé   une douche

la cuisine

le salon

la salle à manger

la salle de bains

la chambre d'Izzy

Key facts

Make sure you understand and can use the following phrases.

Décris ta maison *Describe your house*
J'habite dans... *I live in...*
  une grande/petite maison *a large/small house*
  un appartement *a flat*
  une ferme *a farm*
Combien de pièces y a-t-il? *How many rooms are there?*
Chez moi, il y a six pièces *In my home there are six rooms*
Dans ma chambre *In my room*
  il y a un/une... *there is a...*
  il y a des... *there are some...*

silent **x**	**x** sounds like a **z**
deux cuisines	deu**x** ordinateurs
six chambres	si**x** armoires
dix maisons	di**x** appartements

DID YOU KNOW?

The number **six** is pronounced differently depending on whether the next word starts with a consonant or a vowel.
When it is followed by a consonant, don't pronounce the x at all.
When it is followed by a vowel, run the two words together and pronounce the x as if it were a **z**.
Do the same with **deux** and **dix**.

Test your knowledge 1

 Speaking

1 Say what your name is.

2 Say how old you are.

3 Say where you live.

4 Say one thing about your personality.

5 Say whether you have sisters/brothers or if you are an only child.

6 Say what one of your parents is called.

7 Say where at least one of them lives.

8 Say you live in a large house.

9 Say you've got two bathrooms.

10 Say there is a television in your bedroom.

(10 marks)

 Reading

This is a French girl's description of herself. Read it, then answer the questions below.

> Je m'appelle Aurélie. J'habite à Paris. Je suis sportive et, en été, je joue au tennis tous les jours. En hiver, je préfère jouer au badminton.
>
> J'ai quinze ans. J'ai deux sœurs qui s'appellent Estelle et Marie. Estelle est assez timide et Marie est très amusante.
>
> Je suis assez grande et j'ai les yeux marron et les cheveux bruns.

1 Is this person's name Paris or Aurélie? ....

2 How does she describe herself? ....

3 What is her sister Estelle like? ....

4 What colour are her eyes? ....

(4 marks)

Reading

Read the extract below from an e-mail and answer the questions that follow.

> **Boîte de réception** *[Inbox]*
>
> **Objet: Ma famille** *[Subject]*
>
> Je n'ai pas de sœur, mais j'ai un frère. Il s'appelle Raphaël. Il a 29 ans et il est marié. Sa femme s'appelle Sophie. Elle est très jolie, elle a les yeux verts et les cheveux longs et blonds. Ils habitent en ville, dans un petit appartement.

5 How old is Raphaël? ....

6 Who is Sophie? ....

7 Where do they live? ....

(3 marks)

Reading

Read this extract from a home makeover magazine.

Can you find the following words in the article? Give the French words and their English equivalents.

8 two rooms ....

9 two items of furniture ....

> La chambre devrait être un lieu calme avec des murs blancs ou vert pâle peut-être. Dans le salon, il devrait y avoir seulement le canapé, une ou deux chaises, des lampes, des objets d'art et une petite télé.

(8 marks)

Writing

Write the following sentences in French:

1 My name is ... *(give your own name)* ....

2 I'm ... years old. *(give your age)* ....

3 Where do you live? ....

4 I live in a village. ....

5 My brother is called Eric. ....

6 He's 14 years old. ....

7 He's tall. ....

8 I live in a small flat. ....

9 There is a garden. ....

10 I like my bedroom. ....

(10 marks)
(Total 35 marks)

A pet rat, please

Izzy wants a pet for her birthday. Her father has asked her to write a list of ones she'd like and some good reasons for her first choice.

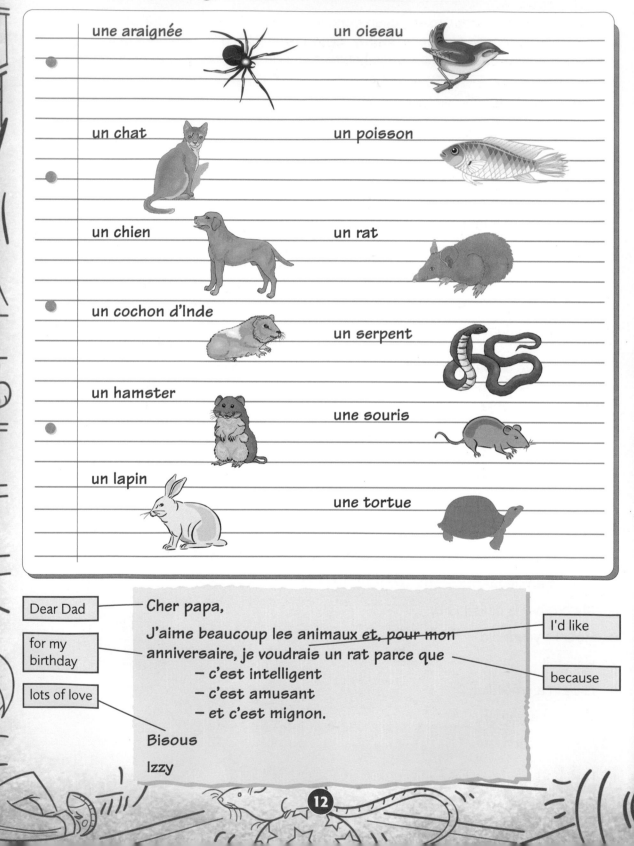

une araignée

un oiseau

un chat

un poisson

un chien

un rat

un cochon d'Inde

un serpent

un hamster

une souris

un lapin

une tortue

Dear Dad

for my birthday

lots of love

Cher papa,

J'aime beaucoup les animaux et, pour mon anniversaire, je voudrais un rat parce que
 – c'est intelligent
 – c'est amusant
 – et c'est mignon.

Bisous

Izzy

I'd like

because

Key facts

Make sure you understand and can use the following phrases.

As-tu un animal domestique?   Do you have a pet?
Oui, j'ai un/une...   Yes, I have a... (see list on page 12)
   qui s'appelle...   who is called...
   qui a ... ans   who is ... years old
Non, je n'ai pas d'animal   No, I haven't got a pet
J'ai quatre animaux   I have four pets
J'ai trois oiseaux   I have three birds
J'ai deux chevaux   I have two horses

Find that pet!

Can you find the names of five pets hidden in the grid?

i	c	b	h	j	l	z	c	s	i	l
a	o	l	s	l	e	k	o	u	c	q
u	c	h	i	e	n	a	i	n	j	a
l	h	r	f	t	r	w	s	g	a	q
o	o	q	n	x	j	p	e	é	r	e
c	n	p	g	t	c	i	a	c	a	é
b	d	e	d	l	a	b	u	u	i	n
u	i	w	e	x	n	j	g	é	g	g
t	n	d	u	d	j	i	a	p	n	i
r	d	a	i	b	a	o	c	k	é	a
s	e	r	p	e	n	t	l	i	e	r

DID YOU KNOW?

**French nouns ending in -al change to -aux in the plural
(when you're talking about more than one of them).**
un animal, des animaux   *an animal, some animals*
un cheval, des chevaux   *a horse, some horses*

**French nouns ending in -eau add an -x instead of an -s
to make the plural.**
un oiseau, des oiseaux   *a bird, some birds*
un agneau, des agneaux   *a lamb, some lambs*

Living in the wilds

When Izzy receives the following invitation from a new penfriend, she and her family are given food for thought!

is situated	in the countryside
you can visit me this summer	I hope
of course	lots of
	we have

Oui, j'habite dans une ferme à la campagne. La ferme est située dans un petit village. J'espère que tu peux venir chez moi cet été. J'ai beaucoup d'animaux domestiques: des araignées, un serpent, cinq chats. Naturellement, il y a aussi beaucoup d'animaux de ferme. On a un chien de berger, des moutons, des agneaux, des chèvres et des vaches.

Vocab file

un agneau *lamb*
un cheval *horse*
une chèvre *goat*
un chien de berger *sheepdog*
un mouton *sheep*
une vache *cow*

Many verbs follow the pattern of **habiter**, so the final letters are the same:

-e for the **je** and the **il/elle** part of the verb,
-s for the **tu** part, and so on.

Verbs like **habiter** are called regular **-er** verbs.

habiter to live
j'habite *I live*
tu habites *you live*
il/elle/on habite *he/she lives*
on habite *we live*

nous habitons *we live*
vous habitez *you live*
ils/elles habitent *they live*

Mix and match

Draw a line from each animal to its correct name in French.

1   un chien

2   un cochon d'Inde

3   un mouton

4   une vache

5   une chèvre

Countryside anagrams

Unscramble these letters to create five words relating to the countryside.

1   **gentnamo**   ....

2   **efmre**   ....

3   **gnariéea**   ....

4   **lvache**   ....

5   **nacmpgae**   ....

Key facts

Make sure you understand and can use these phrases.

j'habite... *I live...*
    dans une ferme *on a farm*
    dans un village *in a village*
    à la campagne *in the countryside*
    au bord de la mer *by the sea*
    à la montagne *in the mountains*

j'aime la campagne *I like the countryside*
je déteste la campagne *I hate the countryside*
parce que... *because...*
    c'est calme *it's quiet*
    c'est beau *it's beautiful*
    c'est ennuyeux *it's boring*

DID YOU KNOW?

*In informal speech, the French often use **on** to mean 'we'.*
***On habite** dans une ferme.*
We live on a farm.
***On a** beaucoup d'animaux.*
We have lots of animals.
*To use **nous** for 'we' is more formal, and more correct in 'serious' writing.*
***Nous habitons** dans une ferme.*
We live on a farm.
***Nous avons** beaucoup d'animaux.*
We have lots of animals.

At the zoo

Izzy is babysitting and has taken Oscar to the zoo. They are counting the animals.

Il y a beaucoup d'animaux!
Il y a … un… deux… trois… éléphants,
quatre… cinq… six… lions,
sept… huit… neuf… perroquets
Il y a aussi des chevaux , des zèbres, des tigres, des
chameaux, des girafes. Il y a combien de girafes?

Regarde le singe avec le paquet de biscuits et la
bouteille de limonade. Il est marrant!

parrots

horses

camels

how many…?

monkey

funny

Numbers 1-30

1	un	**11**	onze	**21**	vingt et un
2	deux	**12**	douze	**22**	vingt-deux
3	trois	**13**	treize	**23**	vingt-trois
4	quatre	**14**	quatorze	**24**	vingt-quatre
5	cinq	**15**	quinze	**25**	vingt-cinq
6	six	**16**	seize	**26**	vingt-six
7	sept	**17**	dix-sept	**27**	vingt-sept
8	huit	**18**	dix-huit	**28**	vingt-huit
9	neuf	**19**	dix-neuf	**29**	vingt-neuf
10	dix	**20**	vingt	**30**	trente

Can you say them all?
Can you count down
from 10 to 1?
Then from 20 to 1?
… without looking?!

How much?

Do the sums and write the answers in numbers and then in words.

1 dix + douze = ☐ ....

2 treize + dix-sept = ☐ ....

3 cinq + dix-huit = ☐ ....

4 onze + seize = ☐ ....

5 huit + neuf = ☐ ....

Key facts

It is useful to be able to say quantities, so remember the following examples.

beaucoup de carottes *lots of carrots, a lot of carrots*
un kilo de pommes *a kilo of apples*
un paquet de chips *a packet of crisps*
une bouteille d'eau *a bottle of water*

How much food and drink?

Fill in the gaps using one of the quantities from the *Key facts* above.

Il y a neuf .... d'orangina

douze .... de biscuits

deux .... de tomates

et .... de fruits

Bon appétit!

Test your knowledge 2

 Speaking

Can you say the following things? (Even if they don't apply to you personally.)

1 I don't have any pets.

2 I have a cat and a dog.

3 My cat is black and intelligent.

4 My dog's name is Tess.

5 I live by the sea.

6 I live in the mountains.

7 The countryside is beautiful.

8 There are lots of animals.

9 There are three elephants.

10 There are ten monkeys.

(10 marks)

Reading

Here is an advert for a lost pet in the local French newspaper. Read it and then answer the questions below.

> J'ai perdu:
>
> une souris grise.
>
> Très timide et mignonne, mais assez grosse.
>
> Elle s'appelle Bonbon.
>
> Téléphone: 02 45 81 81 12

1 What has been lost? ....

2 What colour is it? ....

3 How is the pet described? ....

(3 marks)

Reading

Read the start of a story and then answer the questions below it.

> Un jour Élodie et Michel décident d'aller se promener à la campagne. Ils prennent un pique-nique et ils partent dans les collines. Ils voient des vaches, des moutons, des chèvres et des chiens de berger.

4   What do the two children decide to do?   ....

5   What do they take with them?   ....

6   Do they see any sheep?   ....

(3 marks)

 Reading

Write out the sums in figures, then write the answer.

7   sept + six = ☐ + ☐ = ☐

8   huit + douze = ☐ + ☐ = ☐

9   deux + cinq = ☐ + ☐ = ☐

10 quatorze + seize = ☐ + ☐ = ☐

(4 marks)

Writing

Write the following sentences in French:

1   I have a guinea pig called Fred.   ....

2   I like my cat.   ....

3   My tortoise is small and shy.   ....

4   I would like a rabbit.   ....

5   I like the countryside.   ....

6   The countryside is quiet.   ....

7   There are two giraffes.   ....

8   twenty-one   ....

9   lots of carrots   ....

10 a kilo of apples   ....

(10 marks)

(Total 30 marks)

My family's foibles

Izzy gets a letter from a new penfriend in Belgium.

dear: use *cher* if you're writing to a male, *chère* for a female	

Bruxelles, le 25 avril

Chère Izzy,

Ça va? Merci de ta lettre. Je te présente ma famille.

Nous sommes six: ma mère, mon père, mes deux frères et ma sœur.

Mes parents s'appellent Josiane et Mickaël. Maman est **grande** et **belle**. Elle est **sympa**. Papa est **grand** et il a les cheveux **gris**. Il est assez **sévère**, mais il est très **amusant** aussi.

Mes frères s'appellent Daniel et Marc. Daniel a treize ans, il a les yeux **bleus** et les cheveux **bruns**. Marc a seize ans. Il a les cheveux **blonds** et un peu **frisés**. Mes frères sont très **sportifs**.

Ma sœur s'appelle Katya et elle a neuf ans. Elle a les cheveux **longs** et **roux** et les yeux **verts**. Elle est **jolie**. Elle est un peu **timide** mais elle est **sympa**.

Et toi? Comment est ta famille? Écris-moi vite.

À bientôt,

Kévin

thank you for your letter

there are six of us

I'm going to introduce my family

what's your family like?

write to me soon

bye for now

Spot the adjectives!
Here, the adjectives describe Kévin's family. They 'agree with' their noun – brother, sister, eyes, hair, and so on. (See how the word for 'tall' is spelt for his father and then for his mother.) Learn the tricky ones:

sympa, **sévère**, **timide** are spelt the same whether they describe a boy or a girl.

Key facts

- In French there are three words for 'my'. You have to pick the right one each time.

mon if you're talking about a boy/man or something masculine, for example, **mon frère** *my brother*

ma if it's a girl/woman or something feminine, for example, **ma sœur** *my sister*

mes if it's more than one person or thing, for example, **mes chats** *my cats*
If it's feminine but begins with a vowel sound, use **mon** instead of **ma**: **mon amie** *my friend (a girl)*

- Next, learn the words for 'your', 'his' and 'her'. With **mon ma mes**, it's a simple rhyme.

my	mon	ma	mes		*his*	son	sa	ses
your	ton	ta	tes		*her*	son	sa	ses

So, your sister is **ta sœur**; his cats are **ses chats**; her brother is **son frère**.

être   to be

Like **avoir** (see page 6), **être** is a key verb in French. It's another irregular verb, and therefore has its own pattern that you need to learn.

je suis *I am*
tu es *you are*
il/elle est *he/she is*
on est *we are*

nous sommes *we are*
vous êtes *you are*
ils/elles sont *they are*

Who owns what?

Find the right word for 'my' for each picture and join them up with a line.

When you've finished, say them out loud: "**ma maison**" and so on.

Then change them to use the words for 'your' and 'his' or 'her': "**ta maison**, ...", "**sa maison**, ...". How quickly can you say them all?

mes	**ma**	**ma**	**mon**

maison	frère	sœur	animaux

Key facts

- Words used to describe people or things – tall, shy, long, blue, happy – are called adjectives.

- In general, add an **-e** to make an adjective feminine. Some don't change, such as **sympa** and **timide**, they're the same for masculine or feminine.

- In general, add an **-s** to make an adjective plural. Some don't change, such as **gris**, **roux** and others ending in **s** or **x**, they're the same for one or many.

- An adjective usually follows a noun: **la fille sportive** is 'the sporty girl'. Some, like **grand** and **petit**, come before the noun: **une grande maison**, **un petit chien**.

· TOP TIPS ·

Make it more interesting! Put in an extra word before an adjective to give more information:

très *very*
assez *quite*
trop *too much*
un peu *a little, a bit*

A slave to fashion, moi?

Izzy has just been on a shopping spree. Her father can't believe what she has bought!

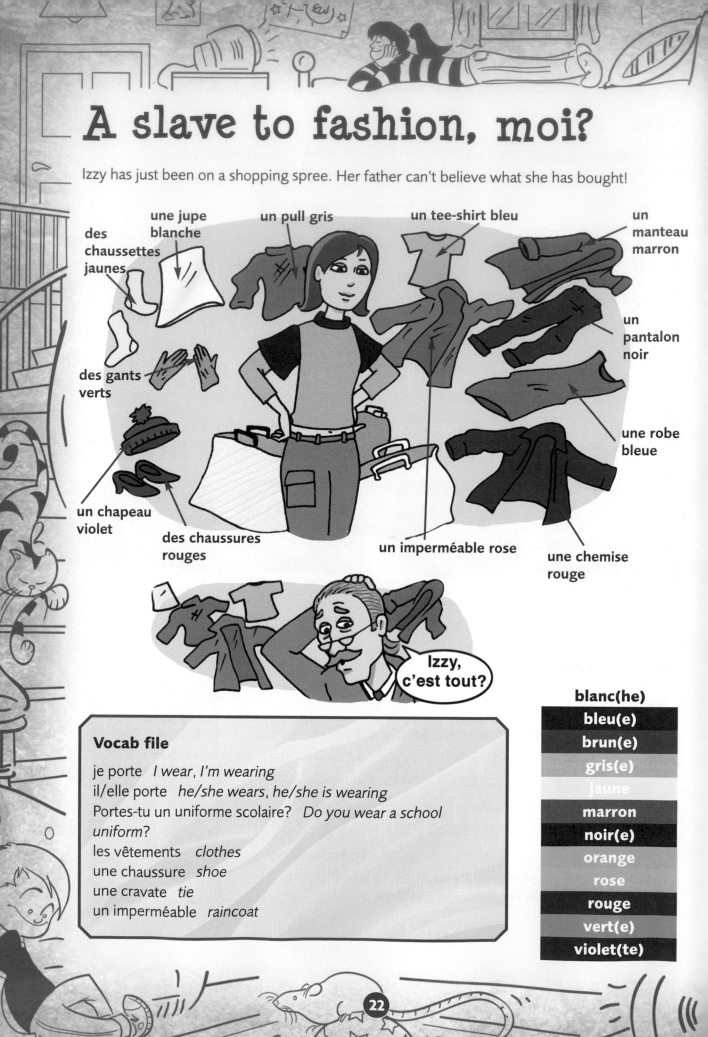

des chaussettes jaunes

une jupe blanche

un pull gris

un tee-shirt bleu

un manteau marron

un pantalon noir

des gants verts

une robe bleue

un chapeau violet

des chaussures rouges

un imperméable rose

une chemise rouge

Izzy, c'est tout?

Vocab file

je porte   *I wear, I'm wearing*
il/elle porte   *he/she wears, he/she is wearing*
Portes-tu un uniforme scolaire?   *Do you wear a school uniform?*
les vêtements   *clothes*
une chaussure   *shoe*
une cravate   *tie*
un imperméable   *raincoat*

blanc(he)
bleu(e)
brun(e)
gris(e)
jaune
marron
noir(e)
orange
rose
rouge
vert(e)
violet(te)

True or false?

Read each sentence and decide which ones describe what they are wearing.
Tick the ones that are true. Correct the sentences that are false.

1 Il porte un pantalon gris. ☐ ....

2 Il porte une cravate rose. ☐ ....

3 Il porte une chemise bleue. ☐ ....

4 Il porte des chaussures violettes. ☐ ....

5 Elle porte une chemise bleue. ☐ ....

6 Elle porte une cravate jaune. ☐ ....

7 Elle porte des chaussettes rouges. ☐ ....

8 Elle porte une jupe noire. ☐ ....

Key facts

Make sure you understand and can use the following phrases.

Portes-tu un uniforme scolaire? *Do you wear a school uniform?*
Oui, je porte... *Yes, I wear...*
   une chemise blanche *a white shirt*
   une cravate bleue *a blue tie*
   un pantalon noir *black trousers*
   une jupe noire *a black skirt*
Non, je ne porte pas d'uniforme. *No, I don't wear a uniform.*

DID YOU KNOW?

**Like other adjectives, the words that describe colour add an -e in the
feminine and an -s in the plural: un pantalon bleu, une jupe bleue
des tee-shirts bleus, des chaussures bleues**

There are exceptions:
**• adjectives that already end in e don't need an extra e in the feminine
un chapeau rouge, une cravate rouge**
**• blanc changes to blanche and violet changes to violette
une chemise blanche, des chaussettes violettes**
**• marron and orange don't change at all for feminine or plural
des chaussures marron**

I want it now!

Izzy and Max have birthdays on the same day and decide to swap wish lists.

LA LISTE D'IZZY

Je voudrais...

un ordinateur

des baskets

une paire de skis

un portable

des livres

Je ne veux pas de chaussettes.

La liste de Max

Je voudrais...

une voiture

une bouteille de vin rouge

des chaussettes

un lecteur de DVD

une raquette de tennis

Je ne veux pas de livres.

Vocab file

je veux   *I want*
je voudrais   *I'd like*
je ne veux pas (de)   *I don't want (any)*
un cadeau   *a present*
des cadeaux   *some presents*
beaucoup de cadeaux!   *lots of presents!*

Key facts

Making verbs negative: an easy recipe!

I like → I don't like
I want → I don't want
In French, you put **ne** and **pas** around the verb. They are the slices of bread and the verb is the sandwich filling.
Can you spot a negative sentence in Izzy and Max's lists?

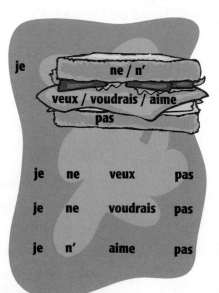

je	ne / n'	
	veux / voudrais / aime	
	pas	

je	ne	veux	pas
je	ne	voudrais	pas
je	n'	aime	pas

Sort the sentence!

Put the words in order to make a sentence. Write each one under the smiley or un-smiley face to show whether the person likes/wants or doesn't like/want something.

1	cadeaux	voudrais	je	beaucoup	de	
2	pas	veux	je	de	baskets	ne
3	je	veux	travailler	ne	pas	
4	animaux	aime	elle	les		
5	je	n'	pas	les	devoirs	aime
6	livres	veut	pas	de	il	ne

☺	☹

DID YOU KNOW?

It's much better to use **je voudrais** rather than **je veux** when you want to say you want something. It's just more **polite**!

Test your knowledge 3

 Speaking

Make sure that you can say the following in French:

1 My parents are called Chris and Jo.

2 My sister is nice/kind.

3 My dog is intelligent.

4 I am sporty.

5 I am wearing a red t-shirt.

6 I am wearing black shoes.

7 I have a purple shirt.

8 I have blue trousers.

9 I would like a car.

10 I don't have a mobile phone.

(10 marks)

Reading

What do the following sentences mean in English?

1 Mon prof est très sévère. ....

2 Ma cousine est jolie et intelligente. ....

3 Tes frères sont beaux. ....

4 Je voudrais un manteau. ....

5 Où sont mes chaussettes? ....

6 Ils portent des gants. ....

7 Je ne veux pas regarder la télé. ....

8 Ils n'aiment pas les chiens. ....

9 Il n'a pas de frères et sœurs. ....

10 Voulez-vous manger de la pizza? ....

(10 marks)

Writing

Put the following sentences into French.

1 My parents are tall. ....

2 My sister is very young. ....

3 Her cat is called Lucy. ....

4 His house is small. ....

5 I'm wearing grey trousers and a white shirt. ....

....

6 I have a yellow raincoat. ....

7 I like clothes. ....

8 I want a computer. ....

9 He wants a mobile phone. ....

10 They don't like the dress. ....

(10 marks)

(Total 30 marks)

School is cool!

Oui, Isabella adore son collège. Elle aime toutes les matières, mais elle préfère l'anglais. Elle dit que les profs sont très sympas.

her school

all the subjects

she says that

les matières   *school subjects*

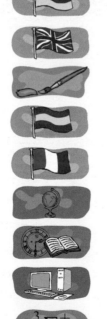

l'allemand

l'anglais

le dessin

l'espagnol

le français

la géographie

l'histoire

l'informatique

les maths

la musique

les sciences

le sport

Key facts

Make sure you understand and can say these phrases.

Tu préfères quelle matière? *Which subject do you prefer?*
Ma matière préférée, c'est le/la... *My favourite subject is...*
j'aime le/la/l'/les... *I like...*
j'aime beaucoup... *I like ... a lot*
je préfère le/la/l'/les... *I prefer...*
parce que... *because...*
c'est facile *it's easy*
c'est intéressant *it's interesting*
c'est super *it's great*
les profs sont sympas *the teachers are nice*
le/la prof est très amusant(e) *the teacher is very funny*

Vocab file

le collège   *school*
le cours   *lesson*
un élève   *pupil (boy)*
une élève   *pupil (girl)*
le/la prof   *teacher*
la matière   *subject*

Finish your sentence!

Finish each sentence, using the picture as a clue.

1   Je n'aime pas ....

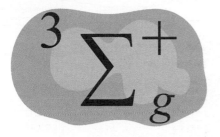

2   L'histoire, c'est .... !

3   La géographie, c'est ....

4   Le prof d'anglais est très ....

TOP TIPS

- The verbs **aimer** (to like/love), **détester** (to hate), and **adorer** (to adore) are all regular **-er** verbs, so they all follow the same pattern of endings as **habiter** (see page 14).

- The verb **préférer** (to prefer) is almost regular, but the accents can be tricky:
  – je **préfère** but vous **préférez**.

- You can communicate well if you know these verbs, so learn them!

DID YOU KNOW?

When saying what school subjects you like, you need to use **le, la, l'** or **les** as if you were saying *I like the Geography*. J'aime **la** géographie et **les** sciences. *I like geography and science.*

Remember that all the subjects begin with a small letter, even the languages:
les maths, **le** français, **l'**espagnol
maths, French, Spanish

School means work!

Close the door!
Fermez la porte!

Listen to the cassette!
Écoutez la cassette!

Look at the board!
Regardez le tableau!

Open the window!
Ouvrez la fenêtre!

Travaillez à deux!
Work in pairs!

Fermez les cahiers!
Close your books!

Qu'est-ce que c'est?

un cahier
exercise book

un livre
textbook

une règle
ruler

des feutres
felt tips

une trousse
pencil case

un stylo
pen

une gomme
eraser

un crayon
pencil

Vocab file

Qu'est-ce que c'est?   *What is it?*
C'est un...   *It's a... (masculine item)*
C'est une...   *It's a... (feminine item)*
Ce sont des...   *They're... (plural items)*

Anagrams

Work out what these are – they're all things you'd see in school.

1 etourss ....

2 ebatlau ....

3 losyt ....

4 hicera ....

5 trope ....

Yes or no?

Read each sentence and put a smiley or un-smiley face after it to show whether the speaker likes or dislikes something.

1 Je déteste l'allemand. C'est nul. ☺

2 Mes profs sont amusants. ☺

3 Je n'aime pas l'anglais. ☺

4 J'ai beaucoup de devoirs! ☹

5 L'histoire, c'est facile. ☺

• TOP TIPS •

It's good to give opinions! Don't just say you like or don't like something: add a reason – "because it's …".

J'aime les sciences parce que c'est très intéressant.

Key facts

These phrases are useful for saying what you <u>don't</u> like about something. See page 28 for the positive points!

Tu aimes ton collège? *Do you like your school?*
oui – non – un peu *yes – no – a bit*
Je n'aime pas le/la/l'/les… *I don't like…*
Je déteste le/la/l'/les… *I hate…*
c'est difficile/ennuyeux/nul *it's difficult/boring/rubbish*
le/la prof est trop sévère *the teacher is too strict*

Alphabetti spaghetti

The alphabet

In French, the alphabet sounds like this. Read them all out loud, making the letters short, not long.

a	ah	**n**	en
b	bay	**o**	oh
c	say	**p**	pay
d	day	**q**	koo
e	euh	**r**	air
f	ef	**s**	ess
g	zhay	**t**	tay
h	ash	**u**	oo
i	ee	**v**	vay
j	zhee	**w**	doobl-vay
k	kah	**x**	eex
l	el	**y**	ee-grek
m	em	**z**	zed

• TOP TIPS •

There is often an accent on certain letters of a word. You need to learn these along with the spelling of a word.

é	accent aigu
à è	accent grave
ê ô û	circonflexe
ç	cédille

Make it rhyme!

Try saying the letters of this name out loud in French. Then pick out two sounds that rhyme and circle the letters.

NB: The letters you pick have to be two different letters!

S-P-O-T-L-E-S-S

And the top accent is...

Tick the columns to show which letters with accents are used in these words. Then add up the totals. Which one appears most often?

		é	è	ê	ç
1	téléphone				
2	chère				
3	français				
4	intéressant				
5	déteste				
6	matière				
7	préfère				
8	très				
9	fenêtre				
10	écoutez				

• TOP TIPS •

- To ask someone how to spell their name, say: **Ça s'écrit comment?**
- When you're asked to spell your name, start: **Ça s'écrit...**
- Go on, have a go now!

Test your knowledge 4

 Speaking

Can you say the following in French?

1 I like French.

2 I don't like history.

3 English is difficult.

4 My teachers are nice.

5 I hate homework.

6 It's a ruler.

7 Say the following letters out loud:

d   e   f

8 Say these letters out loud:

g   j

(8 marks)

Reading

What do the following sentences mean in English?

1 Ma matière préférée, c'est l'histoire. ....

2 Mon frère déteste les sciences parce que c'est ennuyeux. ....

3 Mon prof de musique est très sévère. ....

4 Mes amis aiment beaucoup le français. ....

5 J'ai beaucoup de devoirs. ....

6 Mon cours de sciences est très ennuyeux. ....

7 Fermez la porte! ....

8 Mon stylo est rouge. ....

(8 marks)

Reading/Writing

What is wrong with the following French words? Write any corrections onto the word.

1 t e l e v i s i o n

2 l a   g e o g r a p h i e

3 l e   c o l l e g e

4 l e   d e j e u n e r

5 c h e r e

6 c a

7 f e n e t r e

8 f r e r e

(8 marks)

Writing

Write these sentences in French:

1 My favourite subject is art.

2 I hate maths.

3 My teacher is fun.

4 French is great!

5 He loves history.

6 There is a board in the classroom.

(6 marks)

(Total 30 marks)

All in a season

Au printemps

he does the housework

Max fait le ménage.

C'est l'anniversaire de Ralph!

Et Izzy a beaucoup de cartes de la Saint-Valentin.

En été

he does some gardening

Max fait du jardinage.

Ralph et Izzy vont en vacances.

they go on holiday

En automne

she goes to school

Izzy va au collège.

Ralph joue du piano.

Max se repose!

En hiver

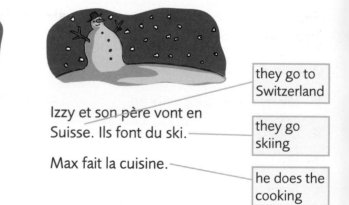

they go to Switzerland

Izzy et son père vont en Suisse. Ils font du ski.

they go skiing

Max fait la cuisine.

he does the cooking

---

aller and **faire**

Two irregular verbs: spot them in the four seasons above!

aller *to go*	faire *to do, to make*
je vais *I go*	**je fais** *I do*
tu vas *you go*	**tu fais** *you do*
il/elle va *he/she goes*	**il/elle fait** *he/she does*
on va *we go*	**on fait** *we do*
nous allons *we go*	**nous faisons** *we do*
vous allez *you go*	**vous faites** *you do*
ils/elles vont *they go*	**ils/elles font** *they do*

Key facts

Make sure you understand and can say these phrases.

Que fais-tu au printemps? *What do you do in spring?*
Que fais-tu en été/en automne/en hiver? *What do you do in summer/autumn/winter?*

je vais chez mon père *I go to my dad's house*
tu vas au collège *you go to school*
on va en vacances *we go on holiday*

je fais mes devoirs *I do my homework*
tu fais le ménage *you do the housework*
on fait du ski *we go skiing*

Which verb?

Fill in the gaps with the correct parts of **aller** or **faire**, using the verbs in the box below. You'll need to use one of the verbs twice.

1 Elle .... le ménage avec mon frère.

2 Tu .... en vacances au mois de juillet?

3 .... t il au collège aujourd'hui?

4 Je .... du jardinage quand il .... beau

fait	fais	va	vas

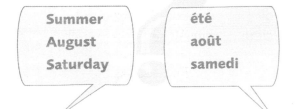

Izzy's diary

lundi, le 1er janvier
Thomas ne me téléphone pas.
C'est énervant!

> it's annoying!

mardi, le 2 janvier
Peut-être que T a beaucoup de
choses à faire avec sa famille.

> perhaps T has lots of things to do with his family

mercredi, le 3 janvier
Non, je ne l'aime plus. C'est
fini!

> I don't like him any more. It's finished!

jeudi, le 4 janvier
Thomas m'a téléphoné!
Le pauvre! Il est malade!

> Poor thing! He's ill

vendredi, le 5 janvier
Je suis malade!

samedi, le 6 janvier
Très malade… Je vais mourir…

> I'm going to die…

dimanche, le 7 janvier

Aujourd'hui, ça va! ☺

Vocab file

aujourd'hui *today*
demain *tomorrow*
hier *yesterday*

On est quel jour aujourd'hui?
What day is it today?
C'est mardi *It's Tuesday*
Quelle est la date aujourd'hui?
What's the date today?
C'est le 5 septembre *It's the 5th of September*

les mois

janvier	juillet
février	août
mars	septembre
avril	octobre
mai	novembre
juin	décembre

les jours de la semaine

lundi	vendredi
mardi	samedi
mercredi	dimanche
jeudi	

Remember! No capital letters in French for names of months and days!

Correct the typing error!

Correct the mistakes in these dates.

1 *le 3 decembre*

2 *la 6 aout*

3 *le 20th fevrier*

4 *le 5 Octobre*

Anagrams

Unscramble the letters so that you end up with a day or a month.

1 emeetsbpr ....

2 imncdhea ....

3 arms ....

4 luletji ....

5 vrlai ....

DID YOU KNOW?

In French, you say "the 5 September" instead of "the 5th of September". So it's easier than in English!

The first of the month is the odd one out, though. You have to say **le premier** meaning the first. You write it like this: 1er

Beat the clock!

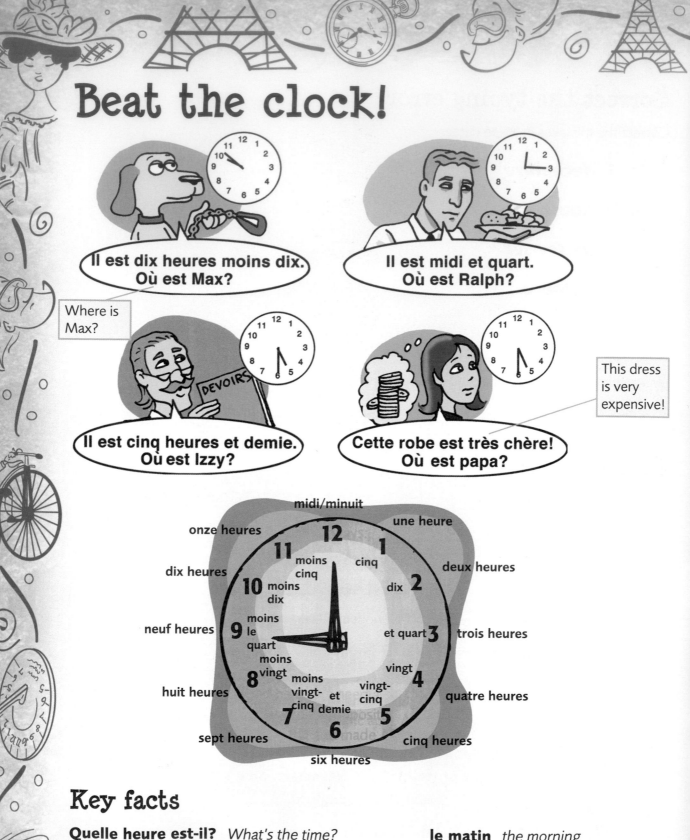

Il est dix heures moins dix.
Où est Max?

Where is Max?

Il est midi et quart.
Où est Ralph?

Il est cinq heures et demie.
Où est Izzy?

Cette robe est très chère!
Où est papa?

This dress is very expensive!

midi/minuit
une heure
onze heures
moins cinq
cinq
deux heures
dix heures
moins dix
dix
neuf heures
moins le quart
et quart
trois heures
moins vingt
vingt
huit heures
moins vingt-cinq
et demie
vingt-cinq
quatre heures
sept heures
cinq heures
six heures

Key facts

Quelle heure est-il? *What's the time?*
il est deux heures *it's 2 o'clock*
il est trois heures dix *it's 10 past 3*
il est sept heures et quart *it's quarter past 7*
il est dix heures et demie *it's half past 10*
il est midi moins le quart *it's quarter to 12*

le matin *the morning*
l'après-midi *the afternoon*
le soir *the evening*

What time is it?

Draw the times on the clocks.

1 Il est neuf heures.

2 Il est huit heures moins le quart.

3 Il est quatre heures vingt-cinq.

4 Il est une heure dix.

Beat the clock!

There are seven words relating to telling the time hidden in the grid. See if you can find them in five minutes!

m	v	i	n	g	t	h	l	u
d	a	e	i	s	l	e	a	m
a	e	m	r	h	v	u	s	o
d	l	i	i	d	a	r	i	i
e	d	d	o	n	c	e	v	n
m	i	i	s	i	u	s	d	s
i	u	d	a	h	d	i	c	d
e	v	l	c	i	e	s	t	v
a	s	q	u	a	r	t	d	l

DID YOU KNOW?

Just as in English, you can also say clock times using the 24-hour clock. In fact, the 24-hour clock is used more often in French than in English. So:

5pm = 17.00 = **dix-sept heures**

4.30pm = 16.30 = **seize heures trente**

8.45pm = 20.45 = **vingt heures quarante-cinq**

Test your knowledge 5

Speaking

Bonne année!

Can you say the following in French?

1 in spring

2 in summer

Bonnes vacances!

3 in autumn

4 in winter

5 the 1st of January

6 the 18th of August

Joyeux Noël!

7 the 14th of February

8 the 25th of December

9 What time is it?

10 It's eight o'clock.

Bon anniversaire!

11 It's half past one.

12 I eat at quarter to seven.

(12 marks)

Reading

What do the following sentences mean in English?

1 Normalement on rentre au collège en octobre. ....

2 Je vais en vacances au mois de juillet. ....

3 Izzy fait son lit tous les matins. ....

4 En Grande-Bretagne, il neige en hiver. ....

5 l'après-midi ....

6 tous les soirs ....

7 À sept heures, je prends le petit déjeuner. ....

8 Il est dix-neuf heures. ....

9 le quatorze juillet ....

10 mardi le cinq novembre ....

(10 marks)

Writing

Write the following sentences in French:

1 I do my homework.

....

2 He does the housework.

....

3 You go to school. *(use the 'tu' form)*

....

4 They go to the cinema.

....

5 It's Monday.

....

6 Today, it's Saturday.

....

7 My birthday is... *(give your birthday)*

....

8 The 1st of August.

....

9 It's ten to one.

....

10 It's twenty past nine.

....

11 It's half past three.

....

12 At 11.15.

....

(12 marks)

(Total 34 marks)

Questions, questions!

If you leave the house without telling anyone where you're going, expect to be bombarded with questions!

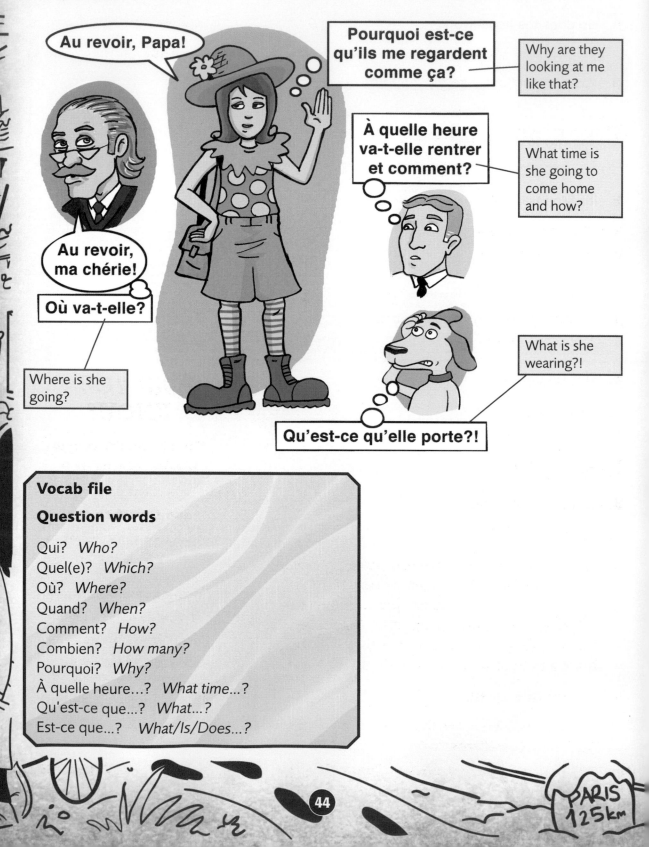

Au revoir, Papa!

Pourquoi est-ce qu'ils me regardent comme ça?

Why are they looking at me like that?

À quelle heure va-t-elle rentrer et comment?

What time is she going to come home and how?

Au revoir, ma chérie!

Où va-t-elle?

Where is she going?

Qu'est-ce qu'elle porte?!

What is she wearing?!

Vocab file

Question words

Qui? *Who?*
Quel(e)? *Which?*
Où? *Where?*
Quand? *When?*
Comment? *How?*
Combien? *How many?*
Pourquoi? *Why?*
À quelle heure…? *What time…?*
Qu'est-ce que…? *What…?*
Est-ce que…? *What/Is/Does…?*

PARIS 125km

Fill the gap

Fill in the gaps with a question word from the list on page 44.

Clue: the first letter is given after each one.

1 .... habites-tu? **o**

2 .... est cette fille? **q**

3 .... est la date aujourd'hui? **q**

4 C'est .... , cette jupe? **c**

5 C'est .... , ton anniversaire? **q**

6 .... t'appelles-tu? **c**

7 .... âge as-tu? **q**

Which one makes sense?

Read the answer, then tick the right question for each one: is it A or B?

1 Oui, le crayon est rouge.

A Est-ce que le crayon est rouge? ☐

B Où est mon crayon? ☐

2 Elle joue au football.

A Où habite-t-elle? ☐

B Quel sport fait-elle? ☐

3 Il fait le ménage.

A Qu'est-ce qu'il fait? ☐

B Qu'est-ce qu'il mange? ☐

Key facts

Ways to ask questions

If it's a yes/no question:

- just say a sentence and raise your voice at the end:
  Tu aimes le sport? *Do you like sport?*
- say the sentence with **Est-ce que ...** before it:
  Est-ce que tu aimes le sport? *Do you like sport?*
- put the verb first in your sentence, before the pronoun:
  Aimes-tu le sport? *Do you like sport?*

If it's a wide-open question:

- use a question word, like the ones listed on page 44:
  Quel sport préfères-tu? *Which sport do you like best?*

DID YOU KNOW?

The phrase **Est-ce que** means literally 'Is it that...?'
and **Qu'est-ce que** means literally 'What is it that...?'

So the question **Qu'est-ce que tu fais?** means 'What is it that you are doing?' or, in more natural English, 'What are you doing?'.

French is global!

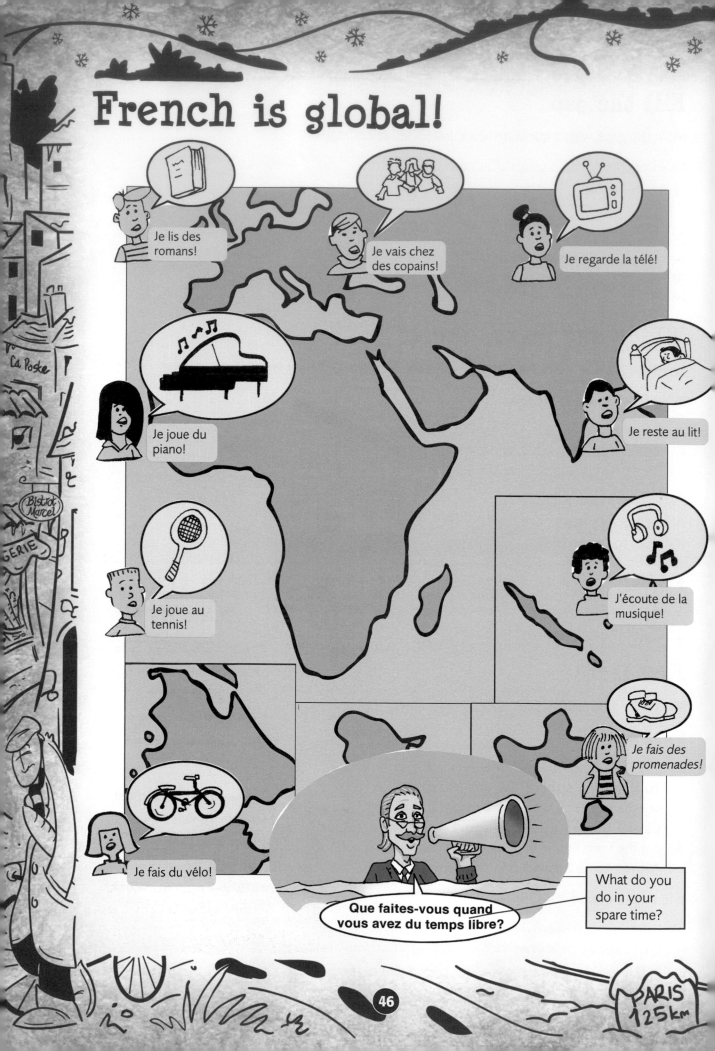

Key facts

Make sure you understand and can use these key phrases.

je lis *I read*
je regarde des vidéos *I watch videos*
j'écoute de la musique *I listen to music*

je vais au cinéma *I go to the cinema*
je fais du vélo *I go cycling*
je fais de la natation *I go swimming*
je fais de l'équitation *I go horseriding*

je joue au football/au rugby/au basket *I play football/rugby/basketball*
je joue du saxophone/du violon *I play the saxophone/violin*
je joue de la guitare/de la clarinette/de la batterie *I play the guitar/clarinet/drums*

You need to learn these useful patterns too:

à + le = au   **de + le = du**
à + la = à la   **de + la = de la**
à + les = aux   **de + les = des**

Fill in the gaps

Cover up the Key Facts and, from memory, try to fill in the gaps in these sentences. Use the words from the box below (they can be used more than once).

1 Tu écoutes .... musique?

2 Elles jouent .... clarinette.

3 Il joue .... football.

4 Elle va .... des copains

5 Je vais .... ville.

en	de la	au	chez

J'aime jouer du saxophone

Je déteste écouter

• TOP TIPS •

You can also say that you like or hate doing one of the above activities: just put the infinitive verb straight after **j'aime** or **je déteste**.

A creature of habit!

1 Je me réveille à six heures.

2 Je me lève.

3 Je me lave.

4 Je m'habille.

5 Je prend le petit déjeuner à sept heures

6 Je me brosse les dents.

7 Je vais dans le jardin.

8 Je travaille toute la journée.

9 Je me couche à huit heures.

Vocab file

le matin *in the morning*
je me réveille tôt/tard *I wake up early/late*
je me lève *I get up*
je me lave *I wash*
je me douche *I take a shower*
je me brosse les dents *I clean my teeth*
je m'habille *I get dressed*
je prends le petit déjeuner *I have breakfast*
je vais au collège *I go to school*

le soir *in the evening*
tous les jours *every day*
je rentre chez moi *I go home*
je regarde la télé *I watch television*
je prends mon goûter *I have my tea*
je fais mes devoirs *I do my homework*
je me couche *I go to bed*

When do I do what?

Draw lines to link up the English notes on the notepad to the matching French sentences.
Draw the time on the clock after each French sentence.

1 wake up	a Je rentre chez moi à dix-sept heures.
2 go to school	b Je mange à midi.
3 1st lesson	c Je vais au collège à huit heures quinze.
4 have lunch	d Mon premier cours commence à huit heures quarante-cinq.
5 go home	e Je me réveille à six heures trente.

DID YOU KNOW?

Reflexive verbs are verbs with the word se in front of the infinitive. In English we say 'I get up', 'I have a shower', and so on. In French you say the equivalent of 'I get myself up', 'I shower myself', and so on.

The 'myself' part of this is called a reflexive pronoun. It's the word me for myself, te for yourself, and se for himself or herself. Before a vowel sound, these become m', t', s'.

Five key verbs:

se réveiller *to wake up*
je me réveille   tu te réveilles   il/elle se réveille
se lever *to get up*
je me lève   tu te lèves   il/elle se lève
se laver *to wash*
je me lave   tu te laves   il/elle se lave
s'habiller *to get dressed*
je m'habille   tu t'habilles   il/elle s'habille
se coucher *to go to bed*
je me couche   tu te couches   il/elle se couche

Test your knowledge 6

Speaking

Can you ask these questions in French?

1 What is the time?

2 How much is it?

3 Where do you live? *(use the 'tu' form)*

4 What is she doing?

Tell a French friend about your leisure activities:

5 Say you read.

6 Say you watch television.

7 Say you listen to music.

8 Say you go to your friends' houses.

Say the following in French:

9 I wake up.

10 I get up.

11 I get dressed.

12 I have breakfast.

(12 marks)

Reading

What do the following questions mean?

1 Qu'est-ce que c'est? ....

2 Est-ce que vous allez au collège? ....

3 Qu'est-ce que tu fais? ....

4 Pourquoi aimes-tu l'anglais? ....

(4 marks)

Reading

5 What four things does this boy like doing?

....

> J'adore aller à la pêche avec mon père. En plus, quand
> j'ai du temps libre, je fais de la natation, de l'équitation
> et des promenades.

(4 marks)

 Reading

What do the following sentences mean in English?

6 Elles se brossent les dents. ....

7 Il se couche tard. ....

8 Elle prend son goûter à dix-sept heures. ....

9 Je me douche. ....

(4 marks)

✎ **Writing**

Write the following sentences in French (using the **tu** form where necessary):

1 When is your birthday? ....

2 How old are you? ....

3 What's the time? ....

4 Where do you live? ....

5 I play tennis ....

6 I play the piano. ....

7 I play football. ....

8 I like reading. ....

9 every day ....

10 I brush my teeth. ....

11 I get up late. ....

12 I do my homework. ....

(12 marks)

(Total 36 marks)

A class holiday

Izzy gets a letter from her cousin who lives in France.

Paris, le 15 mai

Chère Izzy, cher oncle Ralph,

Ça va? Cette semaine, je pars en vacances avec ma classe. C'est génial!

On va aller en Normandie. On va passer six jours dans un village de vacances près de Caen. On va voyager en car.

Nous sommes vingt-quatre élèves dans la classe, et trois profs vont venir avec nous. Dans le village de vacances, il y a beaucoup de chalets et une piscine. Il faut dormir dans des chambres à quatre lits.

On va faire des excursions à des villes historiques: Caen, Bayeux et Rouen. Je vais voir la tapisserie de Bayeux! Le seul problème, c'est qu'il faut partir assez tôt le matin, mais ça vaut la peine!

Je vous enverrai une carte postale la semaine prochaine.

Salut!

Chantal

I'm going on holiday with my class

We have to sleep in rooms with four beds

I'm going to see the Bayeux tapestry

but it's worth it!

I'll send you

Bye for now!

Vocab file

en avion *by plane*	une caravane *caravan*
en bateau *by boat*	beaucoup de chalets *lots of*
en car *by coach*	*chalets/cabins*
en voiture *by car*	un hôtel *hotel*
à pied *on foot*	une tente *tent*
à vélo *by bike*	un village de vacances *holiday village*

Key facts

- To say you're going to do something, use **aller** and a verb infinitive:

  on va aller à/en... *we're going to go to...*
  on va passer six jours *we're going to spend six days*

- To say you have to do something, use **il faut** and a verb infinitive:

  il faut... *I have to/we have to/it's necessary to...*
  il faut partir tôt *we have to leave early*

PARIS 125km

Right or wrong?

Read the French sentences and decide whether the English meaning after each one is correct. Put a tick or cross in the box. ✓ ✗
If it's wrong, write the correct English meaning.

1   On va passer huit jours en France.
    We're going to take eight days to pass through France. ☐

    ....

2   Il faut se lever tôt.
    We have to get up early. ☐

    ....

3   Les chalets sont beaux. ☐
    The rooms are nice.

    ....

4   Je n'ai pas de tente. ☐
    I have just two tents.

    ....

Transport choices

Complete the sentences to say how each person is going to travel. Choose words from the box.

1 Je vais voyager
....

2 Je vais voyager
....

3 Moi, je vais voyager
....

4 Je vais voyager
....

5 Je vais voyager
....

6 On va voyager
....

| à pied | à vélo | en car | en voiture | en bateau | en avion |

Where are they all?

Key facts

Make sure you understand and can say these phrases.

Où est...? *Where is...?*
Pour aller au/à la/aux ..., s'il vous plaît? *How do you get to ..., please?*
Est-ce qu'il y a un/une/des ... près d'ici? *Is there a ... near here?*
Tournez à droite/gauche *Turn right/left*
Continuez tout droit *Go straight ahead*
Prenez la première rue à droite *Take the first road on the right*
Prenez la première rue à gauche *Take the first road on the left*

Finding each other

Look at the plan on page 54 and help the teacher to find Izzy. Use the phrases in the Key Facts to write your instructions.

....

Another day, another place to go!

Read the calendar notes. For each place listed, find the correct symbol and draw a line to link them up.

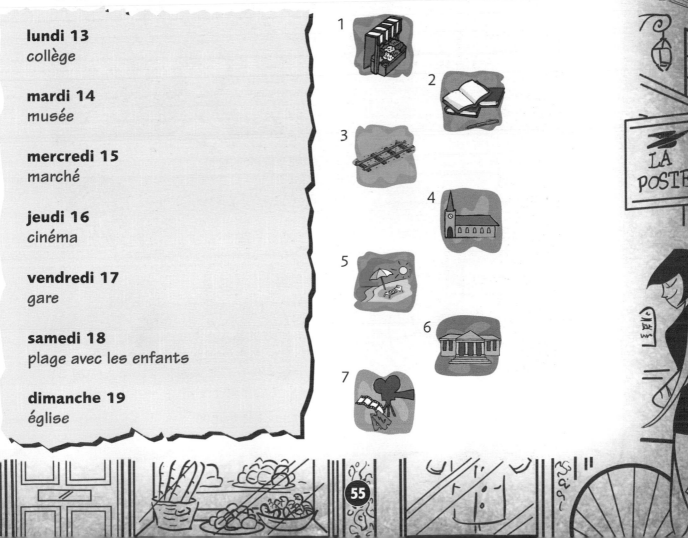

lundi 13
collège

mardi 14
musée

mercredi 15
marché

jeudi 16
cinéma

vendredi 17
gare

samedi 18
plage avec les enfants

dimanche 19
église

1
2
3
4
5
6
7

Whatever the weather!

Ralph loves to get out into the countryside with his daughter Izzy at weekends.

if it's hot
si = if

1 S'il fait chaud

on fait une promenade.

2 S'il pleut

on prend un parapluie!

3 S'il fait du vent

on va à la campagne.

4 S'il fait froid

on va à la montagne.

5 S'il y fait mauvais

on fait un pique-nique.

6 Mais s'il y a de l'orage

on rentre à la maison!

La Poste

Bistrot Marcel

PARIS
125km

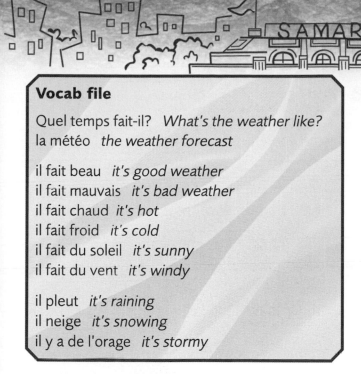

Vocab file

Quel temps fait-il? *What's the weather like?*
la météo *the weather forecast*

il fait beau *it's good weather*
il fait mauvais *it's bad weather*
il fait chaud *it's hot*
il fait froid *it's cold*
il fait du soleil *it's sunny*
il fait du vent *it's windy*

il pleut *it's raining*
il neige *it's snowing*
il y a de l'orage *it's stormy*

Weather report

Fill in the missing letters and then draw symbols onto the weather map to show what the weather's like at each place. (Make up your own symbols.)

1   À Paris, il p_ _ _ t.

2   À Biarritz, il f_ _ t du s _ _ _ _ l.

3   À Caen, il n_ _ _ _.

4   À Reims, il fait m_ _ _ _ _ _.

5   À Nice, il fait c_ _ _ _ .

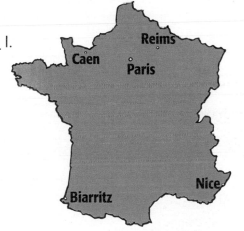

DID YOU KNOW?

Saying "if it's...":
when you use the word **si** (if)
before **il**, then the two words
merge to make **s'il**.

S'il fait chaud, on va à la plage!

Test your knowledge 7

 Speaking

Say the following sentences in French out loud:

1 I'm going to travel by boat.

2 We have to leave early.

3 Where are you going? *(use the 'tu' form)*

4 Where is the beach, please?

5 Where are the toilets?

6 Is there a post office near here?

7 How do you get to the market, please?

8 What's the weather like?

9 It's cold.

10 If it's snowing…

(10 marks)

Reading

What do the following sentences/phrases mean in English?

1 On va passer une semaine en France. ....

2 Nous allons partir demain. ....

3 Il faut se lever tôt. ....

4 J'aime voyager en car. ....

5 Quand il y a de l'orage, je ne sors pas. ....

6 Quand il fait du soleil, je me bronze. ....

7 Quand il pleut, je prends un parapluie. ....

8 Continuez tout droit. ....

9 Tournez à gauche. ....

10 Tournez à droite. ....

(10 marks)

Writing

Write the following sentences/phrases in French:

1 I'm going on holiday with my class.

....

2 We're going to a holiday centre.

....

3 Yes, there is a cinema.

....

4 Is there a theatre near here?

....

5 Where is the market?

....

6 Go straight ahead.

....

7 It's sunny.

....

8 It's hot.

....

9 In winter, it snows.

....

10 In summer, the weather is fine.

....

(10 marks)

(Total 30 marks)

So many flavours!

"Je mange une glace à la vanille."

"Allô, c'est moi...J'ai une double au café, comme d'habitude!"

"Mais, j'ai une glace à la fraise, bien sûr!"

"Oh! Je voudrais une double au chocolat...et un portable, s'il te plaît!"

à la menthe

au citron

"Ça fait combien, monsieur?"

GLACES
simple 2,50 €
double 3,50 €

"Ça fait huit euros, cinquante, monsieur, s'il vous plaît."

Numbers 31-69

31 trente et un	**40** quarante		
32 trente-deux	**41** quarante et un		
33 trente-trois	**42** quarante-deux		
50 cinquante	**60** soixante		
51 cinquante et un	**61** soixante et un		
52 cinquante-deux	**62** soixante-deux		

Numbers 1–30 – see page 16
Numbers 70–100 – see page 64

Tutti frutti!

Draw and colour in the ice cream each person wants:

1   Sophie voudrait une simple à la fraise.

2   Karim voudrait une double au chocolat et à la vanille.

3   Claudine voudrait une glace à la menthe.

4   Robert voudrait une glace au citron.

Meet the costs!

Draw a line to link up the price in the speech bubble with the amount on the price tag.

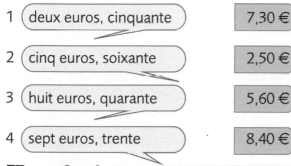

1   (deux euros, cinquante)

2   (cinq euros, soixante)

3   (huit euros, quarante)

4   (sept euros, trente)

7,30 €

2,50 €

5,60 €

8,40 €

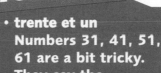

TOP TIPS

• **trente et un**
  Numbers 31, 41, 51, 61 are a bit tricky. They say the equivalent of 'thirty and one', 'forty and one', and so on.
• **trente-deux**
  Numbers 32, 33, 34 and the rest are formed in the same way as English numbers: 'thirty-two', and so on.

Key facts

Je voudrais ..., s'il vous plaît   *I'd like ..., please*
une glace au/à la...   *a ... ice cream*
Quel parfum?   *What flavour?*
Une simple ou une double?   *A single or a double cone?*
Ça fait combien?   *How much is that?*
Ça fait ... euros, s'il vous plaît   *That's ... euros, please*

DID YOU KNOW?

The currency in France, and in most European countries, is euros and cents.

In French, they're called **euros** (the s is silent) and **cents** or **centimes**.

You use a comma instead of a full stop when writing price in figures: **16,50 €**

Remember the difference between **tu** and **vous**:

Use **tu** to speak to someone your age or younger.

Use **vous** to speak to an adult or more than one person.

Remember also the two forms of 'please':

s'il te plaît – this goes with **tu**

s'il vous plaît – this goes with **vous**

In the mood for junk food

Café 'Chez Max'

crêpe	3,50 €		thé	1,20 €	
croque-monsieur	2,50 €		café	1,20 €	
hamburger	3,10 €		chocolat chaud	1,50 €	
hot-dog	2,00 €		Orangina™	1,30 €	
sandwich au jambon	1,30 €		limonade	1,40 €	
sandwich au fromage	1,30 €		coca	1,40 €	
frites	1,20 €				
pizza	3,40 €				

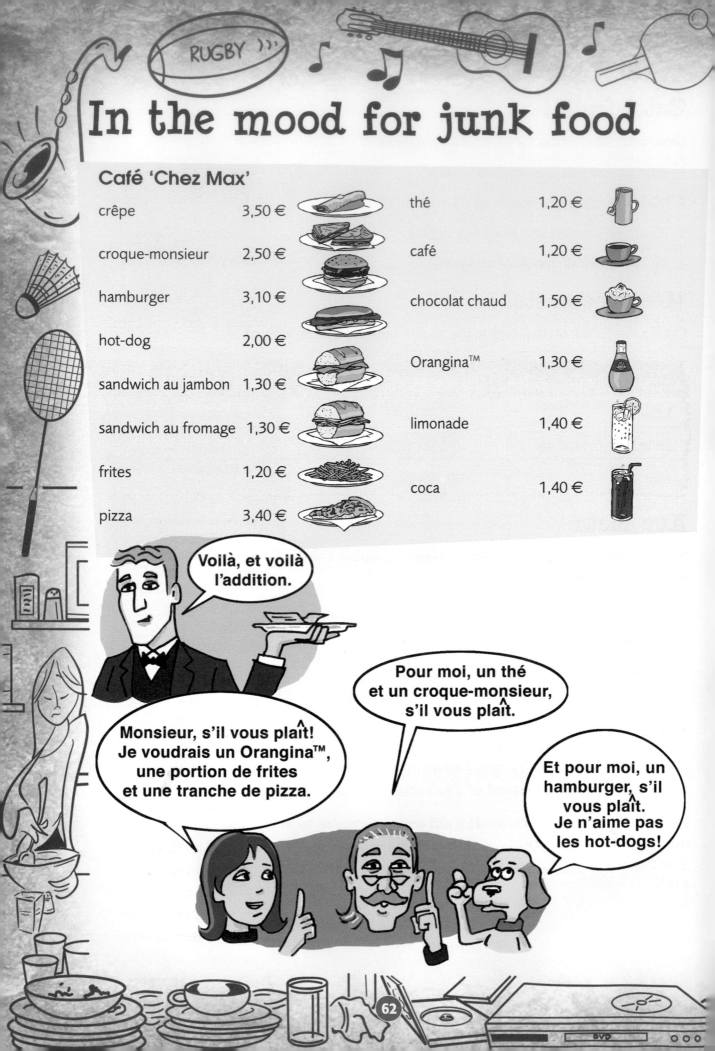

Voilà, et voilà l'addition.

Pour moi, un thé et un croque-monsieur, s'il vous plaît.

Monsieur, s'il vous plaît! Je voudrais un Orangina™, une portion de frites et une tranche de pizza.

Et pour moi, un hamburger, s'il vous plaît. Je n'aime pas les hot-dogs!

Get it right!

Look at the food on each tray and fill in the waiter's list to show what was ordered.
Put numbers in the correct column.

tray for table 1
= 2 slices of pizza, 1 portion of chips, 2 coffees, 1 orange juice.

tray for table 2
= 2 pancakes, 1 cup of tea, 1 orange juice.

tray for table 3
= 3 sandwiches (2 cheese, 1 ham), 2 coffees, 1 tea.

	café	thé	jus d'orange	sandwich	frites	pizza	crêpe
Table 1							
Table 2							
Table 3							

Anagrams

Work out what the words below say in French. Watch out! They are not the most obvious words from this topic!

1   **acerhtn**   ....

2   **tironpo**   ....

3   **dmeilnoa**   ....

4   **thcoalco**   ....

Key facts

Make sure you can say these essential phrases for ordering a snack.

Je voudrais...   I'd like...
Pour moi un/une ..., s'il vous plaît   A ... for me, please
une tranche de   a slice of
une portion de   a portion of
voilà   here you are
Ça fait combien?/C'est combien?   How much is it?

DID YOU KNOW?

Nouns ending in -tion like addition are always feminine. It's a good one to remember!
une portion
la récréation
la station-service

A restaurant? Who's paying?!

Une table pour deux, s'il vous plaît.

Vous désirez, mademoiselle?

Une omelette aux champignons, s'il vous plaît.

Je suis végétarien.

Pour moi, une salade, s'il vous plaît. Et ensuite, du poulet rôti avec du riz.

Et moi, je voudrais un steak!

Vocab file

les boissons (f) *drinks*
la bière *beer*
le vin blanc *white wine*
le vin rouge *red wine*

la viande *meat*
l'agneau (m) *lamb*
le bœuf *beef*
le jambon *ham*
le porc *pork*
le poulet *chicken*

le steak *(beef) steak*
le poisson *fish*
les fruits de mer (m) *seafood*

les légumes (m) *vegetables*
la carotte *carrot*
le champignon *mushroom*
les petits pois (m) *peas*
la pomme de terre *potato*
la salade *salad, lettuce*
la tomate *tomato*

le pain *bread*
le riz *rice*
les pâtes (f) *pasta*
les frites/pommes frites (f) *chips*
le hors d'œuvre *starter*
le plat principal *main course*
le dessert *dessert*
le fromage *cheese*
service compris *service charge included*

Numbers 70-100

These are strange but you'll soon get used to them.

70	soixante-dix	(= sixty-ten)
71	soixante et onze	(= sixty and eleven)
73	soixante-treize	(= sixty-thirteen)
80	quatre-vingt<u>s</u>	(= four twenties)
81	quatre-vingt-un	
82	quatre-vingt-deux	

90	quatre-vingt-dix
91	quatre-vingt-onze
99	quatre-vingt-dix-neuf
100	cent

See pages 16 and 60 for numbers 1–69.

Key facts

un restaurant a restaurant (*in French, the 't' at the end is silent*)
une table pour ..., s'il vous plaît *a table for ..., please (number of diners)*

Vous désirez? *What would you like?*
monsieur, madame, mademoiselle *sir, madam, miss*
je voudrais... *I'd like...*
je suis végétarien *I'm vegetarian (male)*
je suis végétarienne *I'm vegetarian (female)*

What have they ordered?

The waiter has noted the meals ordered by these four people. Which one is for each person: is it a, b, c or d?

Jasmine wants to eat shellfish.
Nicole only eats white meat.
Luc fancies some chips.
Malika wants to eat some meat.

a **poisson, pommes frites, petits pois, jus d'orange**

b **riz, agneau, carottes, vin blanc**

c **pâtes, poulet, salade**

d **fruits de mer, tomates, pain**

Sort the menu!

Number the courses 1–4 to show the right order for eating them.

le dessert ☐

les hors d'œuvres ☐

le plat principal ☐

le fromage ☐

Test your knowledge 8

1 Say in French that you'd like an ice cream.

2 Say the **tu** form of 'please'.

3 Say the **vous** form of 'please'.

4 Say 'a strawberry ice cream'.

5 Say 'a chocolate ice cream'.

How would you say the following in French?

6 I'd like a cheese sandwich.

7 I'd like a hot chocolate, please. *(use the **vous** form)*

8 I'm vegetarian.

9 A table for four, please.

10 The bill, please.

(10 marks)

Reading

Read the speech bubbles and answer the questions that follow.

– Ça fait combien, madame?

– Une double au citron à deux euros, une simple à la menthe à un euro, trois simples à la vanille, trois euros, ça fait six euros, monsieur.

1 What flavour is the double-scoop ice cream? ....

2 Is the mint ice cream a single or a double? ....

3 How many vanilla ice creams are there? ....

4 How much does it all come to? ....

(4 marks)

Reading

Read the extract below and then answer the questions.

> Izzy voudrait une tranche de pizza, une portion de frites et un jus d'orange. Max voudrait une crêpe au jambon et un thé, et Ralph voudrait un croque-monsieur et un coca.

5 What two items would Izzy like to eat? (2 marks) ....

6 What would Ralph like to eat? ....

7 What kind of crêpe would Max like to eat? ....

8 Who wants orange juice to drink? ....

9 Who wants a cup of tea? ....

(6 marks)

Writing

Write the following sentences in French and the prices in words:

1 I'd like a coffee ice-cream, please. ....

2 How much is it? ....

3 I'd like a cheese sandwich. ....

4 3,40 € ....

5 5,60 € ....

(5 marks)

Writing

Write these words in French, starting with **le**, **la** or **les** as appropriate.

6 meat ....

7 fish ....

8 rice ....

9 carrots ....

10 bread ....

(5 marks)

(Total 30 marks)

Snail mail

Une carte postale

a postcard

un timbre

I'm at the seaside

I sunbathe

they're boring!

we're going to see a cultural film

I'd rather stay

it's more fun

lundi, le 24 juillet.

Salut!

Ça va? Je suis au bord de la mer avec mon père et Spotless. Aujourd'hui, il fait beau, c'est super! Je nage, je me bronze et je joue avec Spotless. Mais toutes les galeries d'art, tous les cafés, c'est ennuyeux!
   Ce soir on va voir un film culturel. Moi, je préfère rester avec Spotless parce que c'est plus amusant.

À bientôt!

Grosses bises

Izzy

Une lettre

we've having a great time here

every day, we get up early

What a life!

I hope all's well.

Les Sables d'Olonne, le 24 juillet

Chère maman,

Merci de ta lettre. Je suis en vacances avec Izzy et Spotless. Il fait du soleil et on s'amuse bien ici. Tous les jours, on se lève tôt et on visite les galeries d'art. Cet après-midi, on va dîner dans un bon restaurant. Ce soir, on va aller au cinéma!
Quelle vie! Izzy est très contente et elle adore faire des visites avec moi. Et toi? J'espère que tout va bien.

Amitiés
Ralph

Vocab file

j'ai un correspondant *I've got a (male) penfriend*
j'ai une correspondante *I've got a (female) penfriend*

ce matin *this morning*
cet après-midi *this afternoon*
ce soir *this evening*
tous les jours *every day*

Put it in order

Cover up page 68. Then put the scraps of paper into the order in which you'd see them in an informal letter. Number them 1–6.

a) ☐ Amitiés, Claire

b) ☐ Ça va?

c) ☐ le 5 février

d) ☐ Oxford,

e) ☐ Cher Pierre

f) ☐ Merci de ta lettre

Match the meaning

Draw a line to link each phrase with the correct time of day on the clocks.

1   Ce matin   21:30

2   Cet après-midi   07:00

3   Ce soir   15:15

4   Cette nuit   02:00

Key facts

Learn these key phrases for writing a postcard or letter:

Cher/Chère... Dear...
Salut! Hi!
Ça va? How are you?
Merci de ta lettre Thanks for your letter
Et toi? And what about you?
Amitiés Best wishes from
Grosses bises Lots of love from
À bientôt! See you soon!

• TOP TIPS •

• You must begin and end any sort of letter appropriately. Don't cut corners on this!

• Also, in an informal letter, make sure you ask questions – it can't be all about you!

Now you're talking!

Allô, je peux parler à Izzy? C'est Thomas... Alors, ça va pour le cinéma demain soir?

Allô, Maman, c'est Ralph. On va dîner au restaurant demain soir? Ou veux-tu aller au cinéma? Il y a un bon film.

Allô, Sandrine, c'est Max. Si on allait au cinéma demain soir? Je ne travaille pas.

How about going to the cinema

Key facts

Learn some key phrases for talking on the phone:

Allô   *Hello*
Qui est-ce?   *Who is it?*
C'est...   *It's...*
Je peux parler à Thierry/Madame Leblanc, s'il vous plaît?   *Can I speak to Thierry/Mrs Leblanc, please?*
Un moment   *One moment*
Il/Elle n'est pas ici   *He/She isn't here*

Un numéro de téléphone   *a phone number*
Mon numéro de téléphone est le 03-39-21-53-60   *My phone number is 03-39-21-53-60*

Get their number!

Below are four phone numbers written out in words. Can you write them in figures?

1 zéro trois, trente-trois, vingt-huit, quatre-vingts,
dix ☐☐ ☐☐ ☐☐ ☐☐ ☐☐

2 zéro un, soixante-dix, dix-neuf, quarante-cinq,
trente-trois ☐☐ ☐☐ ☐☐ ☐☐ ☐☐

3 zéro quatre, cinquante-quatre, trente-huit, soixante-quinze,
soixante ☐☐ ☐☐ ☐☐ ☐☐ ☐☐

4 zéro cinq, seize, vingt, trente et un,
quatre-vingt dix ☐☐ ☐☐ ☐☐ ☐☐ ☐☐

Who says what?

Can you tell who says what in this phone conversation? Read the four extracts below and mark O if you think it's Olivia, and P if you think it's Patrick's father, *le père de Patrick*.

1 Allô, qui est-ce? ☐

2 Je peux parler à Patrick, s'il vous plaît? ☐

3 Un moment. Je vais voir...
Non, il n'est pas ici. ☐

4 D'accord, monsieur. Merci, au revoir. ☐

DID YOU KNOW?

French telephone numbers are written and said in pairs.
So a number could look like this:
01 4646 2320 and you'd say: **zéro un, quarante-six, quarante-six, vingt-trois, vingt.**

So make sure you know your numbers to 100! See pages 16, 60 and 64 if you want to revise them.

Email and text - still the best!

Boîte de Réception

Objet: samedi

Salut Izzy!

Je vais au match de foot samedi avec mon père. Ça commence à 11 heures. Tu veux venir? On se retrouve au café Chez Max à 10 heures 30.

À bientôt

Thomas

let's meet

Je suis au café Chez Max. Où es-tu? Tu es en retard!

you're late!

J'ai dit 10.30 au café. Il est 11h. C'est toi qui es en retard. A+ Thomas

it's you who is late

à plus tard = see you later (for texting only)

Vocab file

un ordinateur *computer*
un email *email*
une boîte de réception *in-box*
une lettre électronique *letter by email*
j'écris un email *I'm writing an email*
je veux envoyer un email *I want to send an email*
j'ai reçu un email *I've received an email*

un portable *mobile phone*
j'ai un portable *I've got a mobile phone*
un texto *text message*
j'écris un texto *I'm writing a text message*
j'aime envoyer/recevoir des textos *I like sending/receiving text messages*
j'ai reçu un texto *I've received a text message*

Put it right!

Izzy has emailed a friend about meeting up in town. Choose a word from the box below to fill each gap.

.... (1)

On se retrouve à 10 ....(2) devant le .... (3).

Tu veux .... (4) au café? Moi, je voudrais acheter un cadeau pour mon frère.
C'est son .... (5) demain.

Izzy

| aller | anniversaire | cinéma | heures | Salut! |

What's that?

Give yourself a minute to work out what these important words are. Write the correct French then and draw a line from each one to its matching picture.

1 **aopretbl** ....

2 **tonrrdiaeu** ....

3 **xteot** ....

4 **leaim** ....

5 **teletr** ....

Test your knowledge 9

 Speaking

You're on the phone. Can you say the following phrases in French?

1 Hello.

2 Who is it?

3 Can I speak to Daniel, please? (2 marks)

4 My telephone number is 01 40 20 33 31. (2 marks)

(6 marks)

Reading

Read the following extract from a letter and answer the questions below.

> Cet après-midi, je vais aller en ville avec mes amis. On va faire du shopping et puis aller dans un café boire un coca.
>
> Que fais-tu ce week-end? Demain, je vais faire mes devoirs. L'après-midi, on va faire une promenade avec mes parents. Le dimanche, on mange un repas énorme, alors il faut absolument se promener après!

1 When is this girl going out with her friends? ....

2 Where are they going? ....

3 What will they do there? ....

4 What will she do the next morning? ....

(4 marks)

Reading

Write the following telephone numbers in figures:

5 zéro deux, vingt-neuf, trente-quatre, cinquante-huit, onze ☐☐ ☐☐ ☐☐ ☐☐ ☐☐

6 zéro un, treize, soixante-douze, quatre-vingts, quarante-deux ☐☐ ☐☐ ☐☐ ☐☐ ☐☐

7 zéro cinq, trente et un, soixante-sept, quatre-vingt-treize, vingt ☐☐ ☐☐ ☐☐ ☐☐ ☐☐

(6 marks)

Reading

Read this extract from a letter and answer the questions below.

> J'aime beaucoup recevoir les textos, mais je n'aime pas envoyer les textos. Je préfère envoyer des email parce que c'est plus facile et plus rapide.

8 What does this boy like doing? ....

9 What doesn't he like doing? ....

10 Why does he prefer email? (two reasons) ....

(4 marks)

Writing

Write the following phrases in French:

1 the 30th of December ....

2 Dear Marie ....

3 Thanks for your letter. ....

4 And what about you? ....

5 Best wishes from ....

6 See you soon! ....

7 a mobile phone ....

8 a computer ....

9 I'm writing an email. ....

10 I prefer text messages. ....

(10 marks)

(Total 30 marks)

French–English word list

l'addition   bill (café/restaurant)
adorer   to adore, to love
aimer   to like, to love
alors   so, therefore
amusant(e)   funny
un animal   pet
une année   year
un anniversaire   birthday
un appartement   apartment, flat
s'appeler   to be called
après   after
l'après-midi   afternoon
assez   quite
au revoir   goodbye
aujourd'hui   today
aussi   also
avec   with

beau/belle   good-looking, beautiful
beaucoup   a lot, very much
beaucoup de   lots of, a lot of
une bouteille   bottle
se bronzer   to sunbathe
se brosser   to brush (hair/teeth)

ça va   okay
ça va?   is it okay/are you okay?
un cadeau   gift
la campagne   countryside
ce/cet/cette/ces   this, these
c'est ...   it is ...
cher/chère   dear, expensive
les cheveux   hair
chez moi   at my house
un chien   dog
le collège   school
commencer   to begin
connaître   to know (be acquainted with)
content(e)   happy
continuez tout droit   go straight on
un(e) copain/copine   friend
un(e) correspondant(e)   penfriend
se coucher   to go to bed
un cours   lesson
court(e)   short
un(e) cousin(e)   cousin

le déjeuner   lunch
demain   tomorrow
détester   to hate
les devoirs   homework
difficile   difficult
dire   to say, to tell
donner   to give
dormir   to sleep
se doucher   to have a shower
à droite   on the right

un(e) élève   pupil
elle   she
elles   they (feminine)
en plus   moreover
en   by, to, in
ennuyeux/euse   boring
est-ce que...?   does, will, did etc...?
l'été   summer

facile   easy
faire   to do, to make
la famille   family
une femme   woman, lady, wife
une fenêtre   window
une ferme   farm
fermer   to close, to shut
une fille   girl, daughter
fils/fille unique   only child
fini   finished
un frère   brother
frisé(e)   curly

un garçon   boy
à gauche   on the left
génial(e)   great, fantastic
gris(e)   grey

s'habiller   to get dressed
hier   yesterday

il   he
ils   they (masculine, or both masc.and fem.)
il faut...   it is necessary to...
il y a   there is, there are
intéressant(e)   interesting
le jardinage   gardening
je   I

jeune   young
les jeux-vidéos   video games
joli(e)   pretty
un jour   day

se laver   to wash oneself
une lettre   letter
se lever   to get up
lire   to read
long(ue)   long
lui   him, her

mais   but
la maison   house
malade   ill
manger   to eat
le mari   husband
la matière   (school) subject
le matin   morning
méchant(e)   naughty, nasty
merci   thank you
la mère   mother
midi   midday
mignon(ne)   sweet
minuit   midnight
un mois   month

nager   to swim
nous   we
la nuit   night
nul(le)   rubbish, awful

un ordinateur   computer
ouvrir   to open

un paquet de   a packet of
parce que   because
le parfum   flavour, perfume
parler   to speak
le père   father
petit(e)   small, little
peut-être   perhaps
je peux *(from pouvoir)*   I can
à pied   on foot
un portable   mobile phone
pour   for, in order to
prendre   to take
près de   near to
prochain(e)   next
le/la   prof   teacher
une promenade   walk
quelque chose   something
qu'est-ce que...?   what...?

recevoir   to receive, to get
regarder   to watch, to look at
rentrer   to return, to go home
se reposer   to rest
se réveiller   to wake up

une semaine   week
sévère   strict
une sœur   sister
le soir   evening
sortir   to go out
sportif/ive   sporty
je suis *(from être)*   I am
surtout   especially
sympa   nice

le temps libre   free time
timide   shy
tournez à droite/   turn right/left
à gauche
tôt   early
toujours   always
tout   all, everything
travailler   to work
très   very
triste   sad
tu   you (informal, one person)

les vacances   holiday
le vélo   bike
venir   to come
les vêtements   clothes
vieux/vieille   old
voilà   here/there you are
une voiture   car
vous   you (polite, more than one person)
vraiment   truly, really

les yeux   eyes

Answers

Matching pictures p5
1 L   2 A   3 A   4 L   5 A   6 L

Fill in the gaps p5
1 appelle   2 ai   3 habite   4 suis   5 ai

Who is it? p7
1 Max   2 Izzy   3 Spotless   4 Ralph

What goes where? p9
la chambre d'Izzy: un lit, une armoire, une commode
le salon: un canapé, une télé, une chaise
la salle à manger: une table, une chaise
la cuisine: un frigo, une table, une chaise
la salle de bains: une douche, un lavabo

Find that pet! p13

i	c	b	h	j	l	z	c	s	i	l
a	o	l	s	l	e	k	o	u	c	q
u	c	h	l	e	n	a	l	n	j	a
l	h	r	f	t	r	w	s	g	a	q
o	o	q	n	x	j	p	e	é	r	e
c	n	p	g	t	c	i	a	c	a	é
b	d	e	d	l	a	b	u	u	l	n
u	l	w	e	x	n	j	g	é	g	g
t	n	d	u	d	j	i	a	p	n	i
r	d	a	i	b	a	o	c	k	é	a
s	e	r	p	e	n	t	l	i	e	r

Mix and match p15
1 un mouton   2 une vache   3 une chèvre   4 un chien
5 un cochon d'Inde

Countryside anagrams p15
1 montagne   2 ferme   3 araignée   4 cheval   5 campagne

How much? p17
1 22 vingt-deux   2 30 trente   3 23 vingt-trois
4 27 vingt-sept   5 17 dix-sept

How much food and drink? p17
9 bouteilles d'orangina, 12 paquets de biscuits,
2 kilos de tomates, beaucoup de fruits

Who owns what? p21
ma maison, mon frère, ma sœur, mes animaux

True or false? p23
True: 1, 5, 8 Correct the false ones: 2 Il porte une cravate
bleue.   3 Il porte une chemise blanche.   4 Il porte des
chaussures noires.   6 Elle porte une cravate rouge. 7 Elle
porte des chaussettes bleues.

Sort the sentence! p25
smiley face: 1 Je voudrais beaucoup de cadeaux.   4 Elle aime
les animaux. un-smiley face: 2 Je ne veux pas de baskets.
3 Je ne veux pas travailler.   5 Je n'aime pas les devoirs.
6 Il ne veut pas de livres.

Finish your sentence! p29
1 les maths   2 intéressant   3 facile   4 sympa

Anagrams p31
1 trousse   2 tableau   3 stylo   4 cahier   5 porte

Yes or no? p31
smiley face: 2, 5   unsmiley face: 1, 3, 4

Make it rhyme! p33
P and T should be circled.

And the top accent is… p33
é 6   è 4   ê 1   ç 1   The é appears most often.

Which verb? p37
1 fait   2 vas   3 va   4 fais, fait

Correct the typing error! p39
1 le 3 décembre   2 le 6 août   3 le 20 février   4 le 5 octobre

Anagrams p39
1 septembre   2 dimanche   3 mars   4 juillet   5 avril

What time is it? p41

Beat the clock! p41

m	v	i	n	g	t	h	l	u
d	a	e	i	s	l	e	a	m
a	e	m	r	h	v	u	s	o
d	l	i	d	a	r	i	l	
e	d	d	o	n	c	e	v	n
m	i	l	s	i	u	s	d	s
i	u	d	a	h	d	i	c	d
e	v	l	c	i	e	s	t	v
a	s	q	u	a	r	t	d	l

Fill the gap p45
1 Où   2 Qui   3 Quelle   4 combien   5 quand
6 Comment   7 Quel

Which one makes sense? p45
1 A   2 B   3 A

Fill in the gaps p47
1 de la   2 de la   3 au   4 chez   5 en

When do I do what? p49

1 e 6.30 2 c 8.15 3 d 8.45 4 b 12.00 5 a 5.00

1 e 2 c 3 d 4 b 5 a

Right or wrong? p53

1 ✗ We're going to spend eight days in France. 2 ✓
3 ✗ The chalets/cabins are nice 4 ✗ I haven't got a tent.

Transport choices p53

1 en avion 2 en bateau 3 à vélo 4 en car 5 à pied
6 en voiture

Finding each other p55

Tournez à droite. Prenez la première rue à droite. Continuez
tout droit. Et voilà, Izzy!

Another day, another place to go! p55

collège 2 musée 6 marché 1 cinéma 7 gare 3
plage 5 église 4

Weather report p57

1 il pleut (rain) 2 il fait du soleil (sun) 3 il neige (snow)
4 il fait mauvais (bad weather) 5 il fait chaud (hot)

Tutti frutti! p61

1 single, pink 2 double, dark brown and white 3 single,
pale green 4 single, pale yellow

Meet the costs! p61

1 2,50 € 2 5,60 € 3 8,40 € 4 7,30 €

Get it right! p63

	café	thé	jus d'orange	sand-wich	frites	pizza	crêpe
Table 1	2		1		1	2	
Table 2		1	1				2
Table 3	2	1		3			

Anagrams p63

1 tranche 2 portion 3 limonade 4 chocolat

What have they ordered? p65

Jasmine d Nicole c Luc a Malika b

Sort the menu! p65

les hors d'œuvres 1 le plat principal 2 le dessert 3
le fromage 4

Put it in order p69

a) 6 b) 4 c) 2 d) 1 e) 3 f) 5

Match the meaning p69

1 07.00 2 15.15 3 21.30 4 02.00

Get their number! p71

1 03-33-28-80-10 2 01-70-19-45-33 3 04-54-38-75-60
4 05-16-20-31-90

Who says what? p71

1 P 2 O 3 P 4 O

Put it right! p73

1 Salut! 2 heures 3 cinéma 4 aller 5 anniversaire

What's that? p73

1 portable 2 ordinateur 3 texto 4 email 5 lettre

Test your knowledge 1
Speaking
1 Je m'appelle... 2 J'ai ... ans. 3 J'habite à... 4 Je suis...
5 J'ai ... frères/sœurs./Je suis fils/fille unique. 6 Mon
père/Ma mère s'appelle... 7 Il/Elle habite à... 8 J'habite
dans une grande maison. 9 Chez moi, il y a deux salles de
bains. 10 Il y a une télé dans ma chambre.

Reading
1 Aurélie 2 sporty 3 quite shy 4 brown
5 29 6 his wife 7 in a small flat 8 chambre/bedroom,
salon/living room 9 canapé/sofa, chaise/chair

Writing
1 Je m'appelle... 2 J'ai ... ans. 3 Où habites-tu?/Tu habites
où? 4 J'habite dans un village. 5 Mon frère s'appelle Eric.
6 Il a 14 ans. 7 Il est grand. 8 J'habite dans un petit
appartement. 9 Il y a un jardin. 10 J'aime ma chambre.

Test your knowledge 2
Speaking
1 Je n'ai pas d'animal. 2 J'ai un chat et un chien.
3 Mon chat est noir et intelligent. 4 Mon chien s'appelle
Tess. 5 J'habite au bord de la mer. 6 J'habite à la montagne.
7 La campagne est belle. 8 Il y a beaucoup d'animaux.
9 Il y a trois éléphants. 10 Il y a dix singes.

Reading
1 a mouse 2 grey 3 shy and sweet, but quite fat 4 go for
a walk in the countryside 5 a picnic 6 yes 7 7 + 6 = 13
8 8 + 12 = 20 9 2 + 5 = 7 10 14 + 16 = 30

Writing
1 J'ai un cochon d'inde qui s'appelle Fred. 2 J'aime mon chat.
3 Ma tortue est timide et très petite. 4 Je voudrais un lapin.
5 J'aime la campagne. 6 La campagne est tranquille.
7 Il y a deux girafes. 8 vingt et un 9 beaucoup de carottes
10 un kilo de pommes

Test your knowledge 3
Speaking
1 Mes parents s'appellent Chris et Jo. 2 Ma sœur est sympa.
3 Mon chien est intelligent. 4 Je suis sportif/sportive.
5 Je porte un tee-shirt rouge. 6 Je porte des chaussures
noires. 7 J'ai une chemise violette. 8 J'ai un pantalon bleu.
9 Je voudrais une voiture. 10 Je n'ai pas de portable.

Reading
1 My teacher is very strict. 2 My cousin is pretty and
intelligent. 3 Your brothers are good-looking. 4 I'd like a
coat. 5 Where are my socks? 6 They wear/are wearing
gloves. 7 I don't want to watch TV. 8 They don't like dogs.
9 He doesn't have/hasn't got any brothers or sisters.
10 Do you want to eat some pizza?

Writing
1 Mes parents sont grands.   2 Ma sœur est très jeune.
3 Son chat s'appelle Lucy.   4 Sa maison est petite.
5 Je porte un pantalon gris et une chemise blanche.
 6 J'ai un imperméable jaune.   7 J'aime les vêtements.
8 Je veux un ordinateur.   9 Il veut un portable.
10 Ils/Elles n'aiment pas la robe.

Test your knowledge 4
Speaking
1 J'aime le français.   2 Je n'aime pas l'histoire.   3 L'anglais est
difficile.   4 Mes profs sont sympas.   5 Je déteste les devoirs.
6 C'est une règle.   7 *sounds like: day, euh, ef*   8 *sounds like
zhay, zhee*

Reading
1 My favourite subject is history.   2 My brother hates science
because it's boring.   3 My music teacher is very strict.
4 Mes friends really like French.   5 I get/I have/I've got a lot
of homework.   6 My science lesson is very boring.
7 Shut/Close the door!   8 My pen is red.

Reading/Writing
1 télévision   2 la géographie   3 le collège   4 le déjeuner
5 chère   6 ça   7 fenêtre   8 frère

Writing
1 Ma matière préférée, c'est l'art.   2 Je déteste les maths.
3 Mon/Ma prof est amusant(e).   4 Le français est super!
5 Il adore l'histoire.   6 Il y a un tableau dans la salle de classe.

Test your knowledge 5
Speaking
1 au printemps   2 en été   3 en automne   4 en hiver 5 le
premier janvier   6 le dix-huit août   7 le quatorze février
8 le vingt-cinq décembre   9 Quelle heure est-il?   10 Il est
huit heures.   11 Il est une heure et demie.   12 Je mange à
sept heures moins le quart.

Reading
1 Normally/Usually, we go back to school in October.
2 I go/I'm going on holiday in July.   3 Izzy makes her bed
every morning.   4 In Great Britain, it snows in winter.
5 the afternoon   6 every evening   7 At 7 o'clock, I eat my
breakfast.   8 It's 7pm/19.00 hours.   9 the 14th of July
10 Tuesday, the 5th of November

Writing
1 Je fais mes devoirs.   2 Il fait le ménage.   3 Tu vas au
collège.   4 Ils/Elles vont au cinéma.   5 C'est lundi.
6 Aujourd'hui, c'est samedi.   7 Mon anniversaire, c'est le...
8 le premier août   9 Il est une heure moins dix.   10 Il est neuf
heures vingt.   11 Il est trois heures et demie.   12 À onze
heures et quart.

Test your knowledge 6
Speaking
1 Quelle heure est-il?   2 Ça fait combien?/Ça coûte combien?
3 Où habites-tu?   4 Qu'est-ce qu'elle fait?   5 Je lis.   6 Je
regarde la télé.   7 J'écoute de la musique.   8 Je vais chez des
amis.   9 Je me réveille   10 Je me lève   11 Je m'habille
12 Je prends le petit déjeuner

Reading
1 What is it?/What's that?   2 Do you go to school? 3 What
are you doing?   4 Why do you like English?
5 fishing (with his dad), swimming, horse-riding, going for
walks   6 They brush their teeth.   7 He goes to bed late.
8 She has her tea at 5pm/17.00.   9 I have a shower.

Writing
1 C'est quand, ton anniversaire?   2 Quel âge as-tu?
3 Quelle heure est-il?   4 Où habites-tu?/Tu habites où?
5 Je joue au tennis.   6 Je joue du piano.   7 Je joue au
football.   8 J'aime lire.   9 tous les jours   10 Je me brosse les
dents.   11 Je me lève tard.   12 Je fais mes devoirs.

Test your knowledge 7
Speaking
1 Je vais voyager en bateau.   2 Il faut partir tôt.
3 Où vas-tu?   4 Où est la plage, s'il vous plaît?
5 Où sont les toilettes?   6 Est-ce qu'il y a une poste près d'ici?
7 Pour aller au marché, s'il vous plaît?   8 Quel temps fait-il?
9 Il fait froid.   10 S'il neige...

Reading
1 We're going to spend a week in France.   2 We're going to
leave tomorrow.   3 We have to get up early.   4 I like
travelling by coach.   5 When it's stormy, I don't go out.
6 When it's sunny, I sunbathe.   7 When it's raining, I take an
umbrella.   8 Go straight on/ahead.   9 Turn left.
10 Turn right.

Writing
1 Je pars en vacances avec ma classe.   2 On va (aller) dans un
village de vacances.   3 Oui, il y a un cinéma.   4 Est-ce qu'il y
a un théâtre près d'ici?   5 Où est le marché?   6 Continuez
tout droit.   7 Il fait du soleil.   8 Il fait chaud.   9 En hiver, il
neige.   10 En été, il fait beau.

Test your knowledge 8
Speaking
1 Je voudrais une glace.   2 s'il te plaît   3 s'il vous plaît
4 une glace à la fraise   5 une glace au chocolat
6 Je voudrais un sandwich au fromage.   7 Je voudrais un
chocolat chaud, s'il vous plaît.   8 Je suis végétarien(ne).
9 Une table pour quatre, s'il vous plaît.   10 L'addition, s'il
vous plaît.

Reading
1 lemon   2 single   3 three   4 six euros   5 a slice of pizza, a
portion of chips   6 a croque monsieur (a toasted cheese and
ham sandwich)   7 ham   8 Izzy   9 Max

Writing
1 Je voudrais une glace au café, s'il vous plaît.   2 C'est
combien?/Ça fait combien?   3 Je voudrais un sandwich au
fromage.   4 trois euros, quarante   5 cinq euros, soixante
6 la viande   7 le poisson   8 le riz   9 les carottes   10 le pain

Test your knowledge 9
Speaking
1 Allô   2 Qui est-ce?   3 Je peux parler à Daniel, s'il vous
plaît?   4 Mon numéro de téléphone est le zéro un, quarante,
vingt, trente-trois, trente et un.

Reading
1 this afternoon   2 into town   3 go shopping, go to a café for
a coke   4 her homework 5 02-29-34-58-11   6 01-13-72-80-
42   7 05-31-67-93-20   8 getting text messages   9 sending
text messages   10 it's easier, it's faster

Writing
1 le 30 décembre   2 Chère Marie   3 Merci de ta lettre.
4 Et toi?   5 Amitiés   6 À bientôt!   7 un portable
8 un ordinateur   9 J'écris un email.   10 Je préfère les textos.